INSIDER'S GUIDE

to
Community College
Administration

SECOND EDITION

INSIDER'S GUIDE

to
Community College
Administration

SECOND EDITION

Robert Jensen and Ray Giles

The American Association of Community Colleges (AACC) is the primary advocacy organization for the nation's community colleges. The association represents more than 1,100 two-year, associate degree–granting institutions and more than 11 million students. AACC promotes community colleges through six strategic action areas: national and international recognition and advocacy, learning and accountability, leadership development, economic and workforce development, connectedness across AACC membership, and international and intercultural education. Information about AACC and community colleges may be found at www.aacc.nche.edu.

Design: Brian Gallagher Design
Editor: Deanna D'Errico
Printer: Kirby Lithographic, Inc.

© 2006 American Association of Community Colleges

Community College Press
American Association of Community Colleges
One Dupont Circle, NW
Suite 410
Washington, DC 20036

Printed in the United States of America.

Library of Congress Cataloging-in-Publication Data

Jensen, Robert.
    Insider's guide to community college administration / Robert Jensen and Ray Giles.
    —2nd ed.
      p. cm.
    "Offers advice on the skills and attitudes needed to be an effective community college administrator, covering topics such as the requirements of different leadership roles; hiring and retaining CEOs; and how to deal with faculty and staff, institutional politics, and boards of trustees"—Provided by publisher.
    Includes index.
    ISBN 0871173751
    1. Community colleges—United States—Administration. I. Giles, Ray. II. Title.

LB2341.J53 2006
378.1'010973—dc22   2006034241

*To our friends, colleagues, and mentors
who have taught us, tolerated us, and helped make
our careers meaningful and enjoyable*

*and to Earl L. Klapstein, community college
president and chancellor*

CONTENTS

PREFACE

E very profession has its written and unwritten rules about how to be successful. Community college leadership is no exception. This book is about how to survive, thrive, and make a difference as a community college leader in a political arena that can sometimes be overwhelming. We will share with you ideas, anecdotes, and vicarious experiences that should help you survive the pitfalls that inevitably, but temporarily, set you back and that will help you take advantage of career opportunities.

For example, years ago we knew a community college chancellor who had built a national reputation for educational innovation and service to students. At the peak of his popularity and esteem, his business manager walked into his office one day and announced that the college district was on the edge of fiscal collapse. The business manager had made a series of bad guesses and had been afraid to notify his famous and often out-of-town boss. Now, like a championship skier at the bottom of a hill looking up at an oncoming avalanche, the well-respected college leader stood defenseless as the board, the faculty, and the community overwhelmed him, first demanding answers and ultimately his resignation.

All of us make mistakes some time during our careers. Whether you're a college administrator, faculty leader, or college trustee, or have made it to the top as a college president or chancellor, this book can widen your perspective and perhaps help you avoid getting blindsided like our friend in the story. For college administrators, the story illustrates a theme we will touch on throughout the book: You can be a well-respected leader, be in demand as a conference speaker, and have people calling you for advice, but you had better keep an eye on your own shop if you want to keep your reputation intact. This book will help you focus on the important issues and give you some helpful ideas on how to handle those issues in the best interest of students, your institution, and your career.

For faculty leaders, this book will give you insights into community college leadership and how the challenges of college leadership intermingle with faculty politics. We will also help answer a basic question for many readers: Should I take the plunge into college administration? Likewise, college trustees can benefit from our inside-the-campus look at the challenges facing today's community college administrators and faculty leaders and from our experience on how trustees can best serve their institutions and provide dynamic leadership.

For university graduate students, many of you already new to faculty or to administration, the book is a valuable resource as you think about your future personal and career goals. Much of what we talk about, including the rewards and the downsides of administrative leadership, are usually available only via on-the-job training. We have attempted here to provide a candid overview of the issues, challenges, and pitfalls of life as an administrator.

We have held just about every job in the classroom and the executive suite, from instructor and faculty leader to campus dean, vice president, president, and chancellor in single-campus and multicollege districts. In the past 30 years, we have worked in seven community college districts in three states. We have not only driven the bus, we have worked under the hood and changed the tires, and we have the dirty fingernails and bruises to prove it. Let us help you learn from our mistakes, missteps, and successes.

Terminology Used in This Book

Titles and job descriptions commonly used in community colleges can be misleading. For example, the title of college president may represent someone who runs one college or several. He or she may also be called a chancellor or chief executive officer (CEO). To minimize this confusion, we will use the following designations:

CEO: the chief executive officer of a community college district. We will use the term CEO to refer to the head of either a single-campus college or a multicollege district. In either case, the CEO is the district's top administrative officer, reporting directly to the board of trustees.

Chancellor: the CEO of a multicollege or multicampus district.

President: the top person at a college or campus in a multicollege or multicampus district. Presidents report to the chancellor.

Other common job descriptions referred to in the book include the following:

Board of trustees: elected or appointed citizens who serve as the governing board of a community college or college district.

Vice president or vice chancellor: a second-level administrator found on the campus or in a district office.

Dean: the third level of administration below the vice president but above the program directors, supervisors, and department chairpersons. We use the term to designate a middle-management position. We recognize that at some colleges, the dean is actually a vice president.

Faculty: instructors, counselors, and librarians serving on the front line of a community college's educational mission.

Management or administrative employees: certified and noncertified employees hired by the board of trustees to oversee the operation of a community college or community college district.

Staff: classified or noncertified employees that play a big—and often unrecognized—part in making a community college function successfully.

1

CAREER CHOICES, PERSONAL DECISIONS

It is not the same to talk of bulls as to be in the bullring.
—Spanish proverb

THE FIRST MANAGEMENT EXPERIENCE

So you want to be a community college administrator. Congratulations. It's a great career choice, full of professional and personal challenges and rewards. Before you turn in that application, however, let us make a few points.

People who are attracted to administration are sometimes exactly the kind of people who should not be administrators. Some would-be administrators, for example, have erroneous ideas about status and power. The reality is that in many colleges, the union and faculty senate leaders have a lot more power and influence than administrators or middle managers and are more likely to be wined and dined by the powers that be. Power and status do not automatically come with an administrative title, but, in the community college setting, they are more often the result of the painstaking process of building consensus, trust, and confidence.

If you're a powerful faculty leader thinking of becoming an administrator, remember this: As the union or senate leader dealing with the board of trustees, CEO, or college president, you have leverage. You deal with issues of great concern to faculty. You may even have the moral authority to set the faculty agenda or the legal authority to appoint the chief negotiator or grievance chair or to make other decisions. But when you're an administrator, you are in some ways caught between faculty and top administration. You may be held accountable for your decisions but may not be given the authority or power to solve problems. You have to live with, adjust to, and struggle against a bureaucratic structure nearly every day. You also must learn to say the single most horrible and spine-chilling two-letter word in the English language: No. Or, you may find yourself wanting to say no for the good of students, but your supervisor, the vice president, or the CEO won't let you. That's life in the administrative ranks.

On the other hand, community college administration can be exciting and rewarding, especially on graduation day when the students and faculty and college community come together to celebrate the accomplishments of the entire institution. For us, graduation day has always been a highlight of the academic year. You may have had a tough year with your staff, with the faculty, or with the board, but graduation day is a great reminder of why we are in the business.

Still wondering if you want to be an administrator? Ask yourself the following questions:

- Were you uncomfortable being a department chair, listening to the complaints of your colleagues? That's a warning sign. Don't think about it any further. Instead, stay in the classroom and continue to make an important contribution to higher education.
- Are you uncomfortable making no-win decisions, where a significant number of people will disagree with you no matter what side you come down on? If so, don't consider a career in administration.
- Are you a faculty member used to receiving encouragement and support from your supervisor? Ask yourself if you'll feel comfortable switching over to the other side—the side that gives out the pats, holds hands, and is criticized publicly.
- Ask yourself if you can deal with what we call the turncoat phenomenon. That's when you were drinking coffee at Starbucks with your faculty colleagues one week, and the next week, after being appointed to an administrative position, you're being accused of not knowing what's happening in the classroom.
- Or, is your personality such that you can live with ambiguity and disruption, limited compliments, but plenty of unjust criticism and pressure? Can you deal with the fact that community colleges operate within the framework of contradictory governance structures: faculty groups that want to make decisions on budget and hiring but reject accountability; boards of trustees, faculty leaders, and administrators battling for turf; and state

and federal bureaucracies imposing mandates from afar? Some people just aren't plumbed that way, but if you want to make a difference for community colleges and students by providing leadership to people, budgets, and programs, read on.

There are numerous ways to find out whether administration is right for you. Taking on faculty leadership roles in the senate or the union or chairing the curriculum or budget committee are good starting points. Each of these experiences gives you a feeling for institutional politics and the tug and pull of a campus community—and whether you have the talent and stomach for it. Each of these experiences also tests whether you have the people skills necessary to lead groups and get things done and make people happy doing it. You either have these skills or you don't. They can't be learned in graduate school.

We have a friend who was a powerful faculty leader who also wanted to have an administrative experience during his career. He waited and picked his spot carefully—a dean's job in an off-campus center. He had overall responsibility for instruction, student services, and administrative services at the off-campus center. The center had its own budget, student government, school newspaper, and graduation ceremony. It was a lot more work than being a division dean but also a lot more fun and rewarding.

But there was a downside to this perfect job. Because the off-campus center was 30 miles from the main campus, the CEO and board of trustees kept a close eye on the center's activities, much more so than any division or department on campus. And what they couldn't see, they worried about. As a result, the off-campus dean spent considerable time in meetings on the main campus with top administrators, keeping them informed of the instructional, student services, and budget issues as well as local community politics at his off-campus site.

Then the problems really began. A member of the college board of trustees who lived a mile away from the center began to think of it as "his" center, insisting that he approve all major decisions and make all major pronouncements regarding the center. When the dean became popular in the community and began to be quoted extensively in the local press, the trustee (who wasn't quoted in the local press at all) started complaining to the CEO that the center dean was "out of control." The perfect job quickly became a big headache for the new

WHO IS MORE POWERFUL?

We once worked with a board member who made his living as a divorce attorney. He called up a campus dean who was hiring a secretary and instructed the dean to hire a client of his. "She needs a job so she can pay her legal bills," he said. The trustee concluded the conversation by making a not-too-subtle threat to have the dean fired if his orders weren't followed.

What did the dean do? Contact the president? Tell the trustee where to go? No, he called the one person he knew who could handle the situation—the faculty union president. The faculty leader, who had both guts and tenure, called the trustee and threatened to have him disbarred if he ever called the dean on the matter again. End of calls.

dean as his success and visibility overshadowed the political and ego needs of the trustee.

By the way, if you are a faculty leader, this may or may not surprise you, but it's not a straight-across move from faculty leader to college vice president. Some statewide faculty leaders are convinced they are ready for a campus presidency. But just because they're comfortable giving speeches to administrative groups and the board of trustees doesn't mean they're ready to run a college. It's a completely different job requiring different job skills. Time spent in the lower and middle administration really does matter. There are valuable lessons to be learned working—and struggling—in the administrative ranks.

THE NEXT STEP: CLIMBING THE ORGANIZATIONAL LADDER

As a program director or assistant dean, your sphere of impact—the degree to which you influence collegewide policy and budgeting—is limited. But as you begin to move up the organization to dean or vice president, your sphere of influence expands dramatically. Suddenly, the programs for which you are responsible have significant day-to-day implications for the entire institution.

If you're thinking of taking this next step in your career, professional and political growth becomes most critical. Take steps to widen your perspective beyond your expertise and knowledge in order to sharpen your ability to see how programs and decisions affect the institution horizontally and vertically. By horizontally, we mean the ability to understand and put into context how your programs will fit across the wide spectrum of programs offered by the college and how decisions and actions taken by your program have an impact on the college overall. By vertically, we mean the ability to communicate both up and down the chain of command and explain to others—such as your subordinates, as well as your CEO and board of trustees—how your programs are affected by various budget, personnel, political, and education decisions.

A program director focuses on making his or her program meet the college's goals and objectives. But even program directors can't be myopic. They have to understand the "ripple effect." For example, if you're in charge of the registration office, you must understand the gravity of the problem created if just one student's application is rejected because he or she did not conform to procedure and registration staff did not adequately assist the student with meeting the registration requirements. Over a period of four semesters, rejecting this one student could cost the institution thousands of dollars.

As a dean or vice president managing several programs, you'll need to ensure that your staff understands the interconnectivity of the entire institution. For example, the vice president of student services who allows the counselors and admissions people to sign up students while the cashier's office and bookstore are closed hasn't figured out this ripple effect yet. Obviously, he or she needs to understand how all the parts work together.

One immediate consequence of moving up the administrative ladder is moving from being a tiny blip on everyone's radar to being a giant Boeing 747. Ask yourself: Can I take the occasional fire, the emotion of no-win decisions, or the pain of justified and unjustified criticism?

If you've been a dean for several years and now want to move up to a vice presidency on campus, here's a fact of campus life you want to keep in mind: There may be an anti-[your name here] constituency on campus that would rather bring in a fresh face for that job you covet so much. The outsider often looks better even if no one has taken a close look. Unlike the veteran dean who may have had to make a bunch of tough decisions, the perfect stranger hasn't alienated any staff, faculty, or administrators, some of whom may now sit on the selection committee (see "The Nomadic Lifestyle," page 15, for a possible solution).

THE BIG STEP: PRESIDENT AND CEO

Being a college president or CEO is a job for jugglers. You have to be a business manager, fundraiser, chief policy maven, keeper of the academic flame, hand-holder, backslapper, art and athletic devotee, childcare and technology advocate, a pretty good public speaker, and an even better vote counter. The job is complex, fragmented, time consuming, and physically and emotionally demanding. It's also the best job in the world if you get a kick out of helping an institution do a better job of educating students and serving the community.

The reality is that any style of leadership will work, given the right mix of timing, skill, will, and yes, luck. There are great presidents who have lasted 5, 10, and 20 years, and there are mediocre presidents who have lasted 5, 10, and 20 years. There are successful CEOs who believe in top-down management, and there are successful CEOs who believe in bottom-up collaboration.

Taking risks, being thick skinned, and wanting to be in charge are all part of what makes a president a president. If you're worried about where you'll be 5 years from now, don't even think of applying for a CEO job. Stay in middle management or go back to the classroom. You'll sleep better and so will your spouse.

How can you know when you're ready for the top job? There are a couple of signs. One is when other colleges or state associations begin to turn to you for advice and leadership, or when you are put into situations that require you to lead others—and you like it. Another is when you know your experience and ideas can make a positive contribution to an institution and you are willing to suffer almost anything to help students and faculty succeed.

As you think about climbing the next rung in the administrative career ladder, it's also valuable to understand that the higher up you go, the tougher it is to come back down without falling on your face and causing yourself a lot of pain and embarrassment. Community colleges, unlike universities, don't usually give the unsuccessful top manager a smooth ride back to the faculty ranks. It's something to think about for your family's financial and mental health.

THE DIFFERENCE BETWEEN BEING PRESIDENT AND BEING CEO

We once attended a board meeting in a large multicollege district where we watched the chancellor, sitting casually at the board table, gesture to one of his campus presidents. The campus president, seated at a table in front of the board, stood up and walked around the back of the board table and leaned down so he could hear the chancellor's words of wisdom. The chancellor swiveled around in his big chair and in a stage whisper said, "Get me a cup of coffee, would you, Mr. President?"

During a break in the meeting, the campus president left the room seething. In the hallway he ran into the faculty union president, who was grinning from ear to ear. What, the faculty union leader asked the college president, had he learned from that? Before he could answer, the faculty leader said, "I think what you learned is that you are staff and probably have a lot less power than I do: Because I would not have gotten his coffee."

CEO OF A SINGLE-CAMPUS COLLEGE

Advantages	Disadvantages
• A constituency (community members, students, and campus employees) • Less buck passing, because there is less bureaucracy • You call the shots • More visibility in the community	• No peers to confer with (unlike in a multicollege district) • Nowhere to hide • More accountability • A lot of care and feeding of the board • Greater vulnerability to the board

There are three types of presidencies in community colleges: the CEO of a single-campus college, the chancellor of a multicampus college or multicollege district, and the campus president in a multicampus college or multicollege district. These have their similarities and their differences, their upsides and downsides.

CEO of a Single-Campus College

CEO jobs in a single-campus college are different from CEO jobs in a multicampus college or multicollege district. The single-campus college CEO has a pretty good finger on the pulse of the college and the community. The CEO has staff right there on campus that can help meet goals. And even if vice presidents oppose an idea, a college CEO can still sell a program or idea to the campus by walking the halls and talking with people to build consensus.

Chancellor of a Multicampus College or Multicollege District

On the other hand, if you're chancellor of a multicampus college or multicollege district, the only halls you may walk are those of the district office, which, of course, is no place to build consensus. A chancellor of a multicollege district doesn't have the intimacy with faculty, staff, and students that the campus presidents enjoy. And, unlike the campus presidents, the chancellor has no real constituency outside the board of trustees and district office bureaucracy. That's why many multicampus-college CEOs try to build a communitywide sense of the college through public relations. One common strategy is to form a districtwide foundation or advisory committee to bring in civic and business leaders who can sometimes help a college increase its visibility and build a constituency in the community.

As a result, moving an agenda is tougher for multicollege or multicampus chancellors. In fact, the chancellor's success in moving an agenda depends not only on his or her vision and persuasiveness but also on the degree of independence and autonomy of the campuses and the loyalty, support, and effectiveness of the presidents. If the presidents are team players, the chancellor's vision can be implemented with hard work, money, or time. If the campuses, on the other hand, operate as independent satellites, rotating in their own orbits, the chancellor can spend a lot of time and effort treading water.

CHANCELLOR OF A MULTICAMPUS COLLEGE OR MULTICOLLEGE DISTRICT

Advantages	Disadvantages
• You call the shots • Fewer on-campus hassles (you don't have to worry about whether the classrooms are clean) • Fewer on-campus plays, sporting events, and so on to attend • Fewer town-and-gown activities • Higher salary	• No constituency (and no students) • Difficult to move an agenda without good presidents • Little visibility in the community • Intense care and feeding of the board • Greater vulnerability to the board • Scapegoat for campus issues

President of a Multicampus College or Multicollege District

Presidents of colleges in multicollege or multicampus districts have, in many ways, the best jobs in the business. They get to do all the fun things associated with educating students and running a college without the board hassles. They can even, if they choose, pass the tough decisions up the line to their boss, the chancellor.

Until you work directly for a board, however, you're still on the second team. Many presidents are comfortable with that role and use their title and their college's mission to their advantage. We've seen quite a few multicollege district presidents leverage their title and their institution's name for grants, programs, and recognition on a national scale. We've even seen one or two become better known than their boss.

PRESIDENT OF A MULTICAMPUS COLLEGE OR MULTICOLLEGE DISTRICT

Advantages	Disadvantages
• A buffer (the chancellor) between you and the board	• Don't call the shots on the big issues
• A constituency	• Subject to oversight and meddling from the district office
• Less accountability	
• More job security	• Handle some petty issues from campus faculty, staff, and administrators
• No collective bargaining	
• Focus on student learning and student services	• Lower salary than chancellor

THE SINGLE-CAMPUS COLLEGE

We once worked at a community college that was the pride and joy of the community. Whenever relatives visited from out of state, the family would pack them into the car and drive them over to the college for a look. The college was the educational, cultural, and community center of the town and a place of special pride for its citizenry. The United States is full of towns where the local community college serves as the centerpiece of the community.

Selecting the type of district you want to work in—single-campus, multicollege, small, urban, suburban—is an important part of the career-building process. For administrators and faculty working at single-campus colleges, the support of the community can be a many-faceted blessing. All the resources and energies available to the college are focused on the campus. With just one CEO, his or her responsibilities become clear: Provide leadership to the college and maximize the educational opportunities for students.

The same goes for the board of trustees whose time, commitments, and sense of accountability are wrapped up in this single campus. We've found that boards in single-campus colleges tend to be far more responsive to the community than boards in urban multicollege districts, where campus constituencies are more likely to hold sway and each college must compete aggressively for attention and respect. The alumni in single-campus colleges are grateful for the opportunities the college provides and proud of its standing in the community. The local newspaper, chamber of commerce, school districts, and service clubs can be the college's strongest supporters when things are going well.

The attention a single-campus college garners also means the political and social pressure can be intense. Everyone knows whom to turn to when decisive issues are broached or when a college employee gets caught, for example, scamming money from a student. If things go wrong, the local paper knows exactly whom to blame. And because the community college is *the* college in town, the town's movers and shakers expect the college leadership to take an active role in all affairs of the community.

If you are part of the administrative leadership of a single-campus college, plan on joining one of the local service clubs. Connecting to the community becomes an important part of the job description, especially for vice presidents, presidents, and chancellors. Civic service, whether Scouts, United Way, or Rotary, can provide a valuable link to the community.

THE MULTICOLLEGE DISTRICT

The difference between a single-campus college and a multicollege district is similar to the difference between having one child and having two. That second child, as well as the third and fourth, brings more joy but also more competition for your time, attention, and resources. Adding just one campus to a district changes the dynamics of how the CEO works, how the board operates, and even the jobs of the middle managers. Inevitably, the challenge for multicollege district leaders becomes how to best allocate attention, time, and resources among the campuses. Unfortunately, if campus leaders are so inclined, the process can become even more complex—and combative—if the colleges are determined to battle for special dispensation.

We've seen it all: campuses involved in internecine war with one another, with the district office, or with both; the small campus battling the flagship campus; the campuses battling the chancellor and board to minimize staff and resources in the "nonproductive" district office; or the district office, whose only constituency is the board of trustees, defending itself against allegations of being heavy-handed during budget deliberations, program planning, or facility planning. The multicollege district is also often hampered by a related challenge: defining and justifying its role. Everyone knows what a college president does. But what does a chancellor, whose office may be in some business complex away from students and faculty, do?

Boards in multicollege districts also tend to be more volatile and political than single-campus boards, especially in urban areas. Boards in multicollege districts often are more responsive to internal politics and constituencies, particularly unions and senates. These board members don't hear much from the community but do get an earful from various campus interest groups who also can provide them with money and endorsements when they or their political patrons run for election. In addition, in the big urban multicollege districts, boards, CEOs, and faculty leaders also deal with the social issues of the day.

MULTICOLLEGE DISTRICT ADMINISTRATION

Advantages	Disadvantages
• Districts can offer a wider scope of educational programs and services	• More CEO turnover than single-campus colleges
• District resources are dispersed throughout the service area	• Longer tenure for middle management contributes to bureaucratic entrenchment
• With campus presidents physically separated from the district office, campus educational leaders have more autonomy	• District office–campus relations are divisive and complex, with the district office and chancellor playing the recurring role of bad guy
• Opportunities for economies of scale that small districts don't have	• Politics at the board level often reflect the racial, cultural, and gender politics of the larger community

In the multicampus college, each campus is comprehensive in educational scope and facility infrastructure. The multicampus college generally has some distinct administrative advantages over its cousin, the multicollege district. First, its name is associated with a well-known educational institution. Second, the CEO is seen as the sole educational leader of the district, because he or she leads both the campuses and a district. As a result, the administrative structure in the district office can focus its efforts on managing and coordinating the educational goals of its campuses, not on breaking up turf wars among the colleges.

We believe that many faculty members in multicollege districts think the district office suffers from a bloated administrative superstructure. We've sometimes found that this perception is correct. By their nature, multicollege districts are decentralized, whereas multicampus colleges are designed specifically to be centralized. We don't think a multicollege district needs a lot of administrators in the district office. We suggest you put your administrative resources in the colleges where they can make a difference. Otherwise, you end up having too many administrators and too many duplicated functions.

A multicampus college should be handled in just the opposite way. The central office of a multicampus college has the same functions as that of a single-campus college. Therefore, administrative resources should be put in the central office where they can manage the educational mission of the entire college in a coordinated, efficient manner.

THE NOMADIC LIFESTYLE

For many community college administrators, adopting the lifestyle of the professional nomad is part of the personal price paid for advancing a career. We all know colleagues who have spent an entire career at one college, moving up the ranks, living in one home, building a large network of friends, paying off the mortgage, and getting to know their kids' friends. We know others who have chosen to move with the job. (We have worked in seven different districts in three different states.)

There are advantages to both lifestyle choices. If you're willing to move, the number and variety of jobs available for your consideration increase exponentially. If you stay put, you increase exponentially the chances that you'll pay off your mortgage. If you stay put, you will also find the options to move up the ladder limited (especially if your boss never moves or you have to make a few too many no-win decisions).

As your administrative career unfolds, you will be forced to make a decision on which road to take: Stay and advance up the local career ladder or become a professional nomad and, in effect, cause a lifestyle change that will have an impact on your career and family. The "To Move or Not To Move" chart may help you choose a path.

TO MOVE OR NOT TO MOVE

Moving

Job Opportunities	Quicker rise to top
Professional Accomplishments	Do more in many places
Paycheck	Opportunity to pick best-paying colleges
Personal Career Needs	New, different challenges
Spouse	Problem if spouse is well established
Housing	Tough to pay off mortgage
Friends	Make more but lose more
Your Kids	May resent changing schools

Not Moving

Job Opportunities	Limited to local openings
Professional Accomplishments	Do more in one place longer
Paycheck	Limited to local pay scale
Personal Career Needs	Stability, predictability
Spouse	May be better for marriage
Housing	Build home equity
Friends	Watch neighbor kids grow up
Your Kids	Stability in school and with friends

In a town this size, there's no place to hide/
Everywhere you go you meet someone you know
—John Prine, from the song "In a Town This Size"

Are Small-Town Politics Really Easier?

Some community college administrators think politics in the large urban areas are more vicious than in the small, quiet, rural communities. Don't believe that for a second. In the big city, you can hide a lot easier. You can get lost within the diversity of people and activities. In the big city the politics are more philosophical. In a small town they're more personal.

A college CEO we know in a rural, agricultural area lived through a bitter personal battle with a faculty member that would send cold shivers down the back of any urban administrator. The unhappy instructor, who thought the CEO was a crook and made no bones about telling the entire town, had no facts—only passion, anger, time, and resources (and tenure) to make the CEO's life and that of her family miserable. The campaign against the CEO in this small, quiet community included garbage tossed on her front yard and dead animals stuffed in her mailbox.

In another small, rural town a prominent physician discovered that his wife—a student at the local community college—was having an affair with a member of the college faculty. When his demand for retribution fell on deaf ears in the college president's office, the doctor proceeded to plaster "Wanted for Adultery" posters all over town picturing the instructor. In a large city, those posters would have gotten lost among the billboards and graffiti. Not in Small Town, USA.

Some administrators will say, "But my personal life is no business of the college." Don't believe it. Did someone see you in a bar having too good a time? Why weren't you and your spouse together at the town social? Whether or not that's anybody's business is not the issue. If you don't want to live in that kind of fishbowl, don't take a high-visibility job in that kind of community.

WORKING AT A SMALL-TOWN COLLEGE

Advantages	Disadvantages
• Do a good job, and you can be king or queen • You're a big fish in a small pond. • You have high visibility and respect as a college educator • You'll experience less sympathy for union issues. (Small towns don't countenance to faculty complaining about working 20 hours a week while making more money than most civic leaders.)	• Mess up, and everyone knows it • If your spouse or kids mess up, everyone knows it • Community memory of college-related problems and controversies lasts forever • The CEO has to deal with the problems of everyone on staff, up and down the ranks

We recommend that you hit the banquet circuit if you ever do get to the small town. It's expected of the top leadership at the college, and it's a great way to build relationships that will pay off later when you need help from the community. We also recommend you live in the district or service area your college serves. Inevitably, you will be out and about in the community and the question will arise, "So, where do you live?" It can only help your cause—professionally and personally—if you can answer, "In the same town as my students."

COMMUTER MARRIAGES

Would you give up living with your wife or husband for a job? We know one couple—both of them top-level administrators— who lived apart for 20 years while the husband climbed the career ladder to the top. Another administrator we admire moved out of the house and into a different state to take her first presidency. Extremes? Not exactly. In today's job market, where opportunity and advancement sometimes require personal sacrifices, the ability to be flexible can make a difference in how quickly you advance toward your professional goals. Because so many professional educators are married to other professionals, a dilemma arises when one or the other hears the siren call from another city or state.

This phenomenon can play out in different ways. Moving away from a spouse does put a strain on the relationship. There is no question that even loving, dedicated couples are negatively affected. It takes a special partnership to overcome not only the physical distance but also the emotional separation. While we have seen such separations work, we also know administrators who, when they move away from their spouse, end up throwing themselves into their jobs, believing that going overboard will compensate for an empty house. As we all know, long hours on the job do not necessarily equate with improved productivity or better judgment.

THE STING

We know a college where the board of trustees conducted interviews with prospective CEO candidates and their spouses and were particularly impressed with one of the candidates, Joe, and his wife, Sara Jean. She was a vivacious, intelligent woman who, the board agreed, would make Joe an even better college representative on the town-and-gown circuit. During the interview, Sara Jean aggressively sold Joe's candidacy. After being selected for the job, Joe arrived in town—without Sara Jean. He assured everyone she would be joining him within a few months. When months had passed, an embarrassed Joe announced that he and Sara Jean were getting a divorce. Only later did the board discover that Joe and Sara Jean, the perfect couple during the interviews, had filed for divorce 6 weeks before he applied for the job.

Moving to a job without your spouse can also become a political issue, especially in small towns where a high-visibility college administrator is assumed to be part of a married team. It may be old-fashioned, but in many communities the standard is still the image of the Norman Rockwell family.

2

Thriving and Surviving
on the Job

*The notes I handle no better than many pianists. But the pauses
between the notes—ah, that is where the art resides!*
—Artur Schnabel, classical pianist and composer

WHAT ADMINISTRATORS REALLY DO

Imagine a community college district with the perfect set of board policies and administrative regulations: published documents that state exactly and clearly the goals and mission of the institution; how the board, faculty, administration, and support staff will function; the rules and limits for student activities; how budgets will be balanced; the curriculum and class schedule process; and so on. This set of policies and regulations, in fact, is so good that whenever a decision or judgment is required—even those never before contemplated—college officials simply open the policies and regulations, turn to the index and, voilà, find the answer within. Welcome to the twilight zone.

The reality of community college leadership is that the written policies and regulations fit about 75% of the cases. There are always one or two situations a week that you won't find in the book. Administrators are paid to adjudicate the gray areas and clarify the ambiguities—the other 25%.

How to accomplish this task? Begin with the personal core values addressed beginning on page 44. Ethical and consistent behavior builds integrity, which in turn fosters trust and a willingness on the part of people to respect your judgment. When you are new to a job, a good first step is to talk with your boss, peers, and subordinates to find out the typical points of dispute and disagreement at your college or in your particular area. Any job has dozens of responsibilities, but usually two or three issues regularly fall within the gray areas and must be handled tactfully. Don't ever assume you already know what all these issues are. That's a good way to get derailed early in your job.

When adjudicating the gray areas and clarifying the ambiguities, administrators and leaders would do well to follow these simple rules:

- Understand and embrace the notion that the bureaucracy's purpose is to facilitate the education process, not to impede it. In other words, don't get hung up on process.
- Take charge. Risk the wrath of the people upstairs to get things done for faculty, staff, and students.
- Take a commonsense approach to decision making. Don't, for example, reject a student's application because he or she hasn't dotted all the *i*s and crossed all the *t*s.
- Understand that the real action at a community college takes place at the department and division levels and that administrators are responsible for setting a tone that encourages teaching and learning.

The fourth bullet is particularly important. The effectiveness of the division and department leadership is critical to the college CEO or president (see page 28). Too often the perception of how things are going at a college mistakenly begins and ends at the door of the top tier of campus leadership. Vice presidents, presidents, and CEOs would serve themselves well by placing a framed copy of the following statement in the middle of their desks as a friendly reminder of where most of their real problems actually begin:

What we perceive in upper management as small-potato issues are often perceived as big, hot potatoes in faculty offices.

Too many managers worry that their employees will make big mistakes if given too much leeway or authority to make decisions. They're wrong. We believe 95% of the staff will do the right thing, especially if the administrator has done his or her job as a teacher and mentor. Perhaps 5% will not demonstrate good judgment or act responsibly, and these you do have to watch.

Building Bridges, Burning Bridges

Have you noticed how frequently community college presidents and administrators move from one state to another for job opportunities? Or from one college to another within the same state? We've talked with presidents, for example, who have worked in four or five different states during a 30-year career. We certainly know administrators who have worked at several colleges within the same state or even region. This phenomenon reminds us that the community we work and live in is very small.

As you begin your career, strive to build relationships that will benefit and not hurt you. When you go to a conference or participate on a committee, and especially when working with colleagues on your own campus, don't ever forget that of the many people with whom you interact during an academic year, it's inevitable that one or more may have a significant impact on your career someday in the future. Someday, one or more of the same people serving with you on an accreditation team or attending a state or national conference could be a member of the hiring committee you're sitting before when you seek your next promotion. One of them could even be your boss in your next job.

Because you never know exactly who will appear in your future in such a key role professionally, it's a good idea always to strive to build bridges, not burn them. Getting on the wrong side of too many people early in your career could wind up sinking it before it gets off the ground.

Being part of management doesn't mean you have a hammer
in your hand and everything you see is a nail.
—Robert Jensen

Honing Your People Skills

The trend toward greater participation in campus decision making demands that administrators and faculty work together honestly and respectfully, even if from their perspectives they find each other difficult to work with.

Do not be like the CEO who let the relentless pressure of a campus dissident cloud her judgment and seriously hurt her credibility. The CEO had been taking intense criticism from a faculty member who was sending out anonymous campuswide newsletters packed with denunciations of the CEO. When these newsletters began to attack the CEO's spouse, the CEO, with the blessings of the board, hired a private investigator to uncover the culprit. Using a handwriting sample from the attack newsletter, the private investigator scoured the campus personnel files until he was able to match the sample with an old application form. The cowardly critic was unmasked! But the reaction wasn't what the CEO expected at all. The campus exploded in anger at the CEO and the board, demanding the "restoration of free speech" and an end to "dictatorial strong-arm tactics."

As you move up the administrative ranks, you will come to realize that community college administration boils down to the inescapable fact that, in the end, it's all about people—how you treat them, how you react to them, and how you work with them. This means several things:

- Don't take everything personally. Particularly, do not overreact to a handful of malcontents on campus. It will just stir up and possibly alienate all the people in the middle.
- Keep your door open. People should come first. Take your work home if you have to.
- Resist the temptation to be on every committee and to run off to every conference. Keep your eye on the ball at home.
- Be consistent and fair.
- Listen, listen, and listen some more.
- Socialize with your colleagues. If you play golf, find some golfing partners from the faculty and administrative staff. If you play bridge, find bridge players on campus.

We guarantee you'll have fewer personnel problems or shared governance disputes if your door is always open and if you listen, show interest, and put your cards (as many as possible) on the table. Too often administrators, like the Wizard of Oz, hide behind a curtain of paperwork and committee meetings to the detriment of faculty, students, and staff.

We were once standing in line to check baggage at an airline and watched in horror as a man in front of us gave the luggage handler in the airport a lot of grief. We mean a *lot* of grief, berating and browbeating the poor handler about how he'd allegedly been subjected to the airline's lousy service. When the passenger finally left in a huff and it was our turn, we asked the baggage handler how he could put up with such treatment. The handler said matter-of-factly, "He's going to Chicago, but his luggage is going to Japan." The baggage handler didn't get mad; he got even.

The moral: Whether it's your boss or your employees, treating people with a little kindness is important. We all know how small this big round planet is and that treating people as second-class citizens is a dangerous game, whether it's your boss or your secretary.

The first thing you learn when you become an administrator,
especially if you're coming from the faculty ranks, is that
the First Amendment no longer applies.
—Pat Kirklin, retired faculty union leader and administrator

THERE IS NO "MIDDLE" IN MIDDLE MANAGEMENT

We hear people say, "Middle management is tough because you're caught in the middle between faculty and the president." Directors and deans complain, "I'm being pulled by faculty and staff in one direction and my boss and the CEO in another. I'm caught in the middle!" The fact is there is no "middle" in middle management.

As you walk across that line into administration, you don't cross over a wide tract of no-man's-land dubbed "middle ground." You made a choice, and in doing so you lost your autonomy and some of your professional and personal freedoms. If there are any tugs and pulls in loyalties, priorities, or goals, they are all in your mind, not in your job description. Your job description says "administration." Welcome to the club.

Now get out there and stretch: Far too often, administrators move up the ranks through either instruction or student services or finance with little cross-fertilization in terms of professional experiences. It's a rare CEO who mentors his or her staff by shuffling the deck occasionally and making the players put on different hats and thus learn new skills. If you find yourself becoming a limited expert (in student services, for example), do some cross-fertilization on your own by attending conferences of the instructional folks or business officials. This will give you a sense not only of the issues on their front burner but also of the potential impact on your area of issues coming from outside your bailiwick.

DIVISION AND DEPARTMENT LEADERSHIP

The division dean—the classic middle management position in a community college—has a huge influence on the success or failure of a CEO. One reason is the morale and perceptions of the institution depend on how well the department and division leadership interact with faculty. You, as a college president, can be extremely popular or successful. The board can love you. So can the Kiwanis Club. But if the science department hates their dean and there's a war being fought down at the other end of campus, someone will inevitably ask the science faculty, "What's morale like in this institution?" and they're going to shout, "It's terrible!" Suddenly the instructional vice president and the CEO have a big problem.

Another reason the division dean is important is that the heart of any community college is its class schedule—the purview of division leadership. The class schedule determines whether a college is meeting its education mission and is accessible by the community. The class schedule also drives the budget. The toughest job a division dean has is developing a class schedule and deciding which classes will be offered and when. Faculty members can be persistent when it comes to teaching the classes they want on the dates and times they want. The dean may be tempted to delegate this responsibility, often to a department chair. The class schedule, however, should serve student needs and not be built solely around instructor convenience. Therefore, you have to hire division deans who are tough enough not to cave in to inappropriate or costly instructor demands.

Maybe one of the reasons online courses have become so popular is because we've thrown up so many barriers and inconveniences for students through our on-campus class schedule. If too many students gravitate to online classes, someday someone—like the state governor—may ask, "Why do we need this big campus and expensive staff?" The college CEO who delegates the hiring of these frontline administrators to his vice presidents misses an opportunity to protect his own best interests; more important, he misses the chance to help set the course for the institution's future. The legacy of a college CEO is not bricks and mortar. It's people.

Where is the knowledge we have lost in information?
—T. S. Eliot

COMMUNICATION ON CAMPUS

An important role for any administrator on a community college campus is communicating up the line with senior leadership, across the organization with fellow middle managers, and down the line with staff and faculty. Middle management acts somewhat like the server in a computer network. It works as the link through which data, dialogue, information, and opinions travel from one end of the campus to the other. The information that management provides through the campus network must be accurate and complete, and the opinions communicated must be based on good judgment.

Good communication also requires that management's professional relationships with faculty, staff, and senior management are solid. Your word will be heard and taken seriously only if you are, first of all, trusted and respected. Being liked also helps. (Having a personal rapport with your staff is like money in the bank when tough news needs to be delivered.)

How can you as a manager obtain accurate information? Assume that the table of organization acts like a communication filtration system. As information is passed around, people tend to put a coat of sugar—or vinegar—on it as it befits their own political, professional, and personal interests. Therefore, you must constantly check to guarantee the accuracy of the information you receive and the information you pass along.

Here are some things to remember about communication:

- Communication is keeping employees and the boss informed on an ongoing basis.

- Deans should constantly communicate with faculty and staff to ensure the accuracy of their own perceptions.
- *Data* is not equivalent to *information.*
- E-mails and memos are both forms of passive communication and are not a substitute for in-person, active interaction.

Delivering bad news to the president or your immediate supervisor becomes a tough but essential role for the college manager. Your boss needs to hear it from you before he hears it from them. And what about bad news regarding the CEO or one of his pet projects? It may be uncomfortable to tell the boss "this isn't playing well with the troops," but it's part of your job, just as it is part of the president's job to listen and learn.

Putting the other shoe on, as a supervisor or CEO receiving bad news, it helps if you do not come off as defensive and paranoid. A boss who shoots the messenger will quickly get shut off from the flow of information. In the preface of this book, we told the story of a highly respected community college leader who was blindsided by some bad news that ended up costing him his reputation and job. He had become one of those bosses who often shot the bearers of bad news. As a result, the business manager, who had prayed he'd never have to deliver the bad news, held on to the time bomb until it finally exploded all over everyone. Consider some other important communication points:

- The less your administrative team communicates with the campus community, the more power the gossipers and dissidents wield within the organization.
- Too many administrators spend too much of their time in meetings whining about the way things are going and then when the president walks in the room suddenly suffer from amnesia and talk about how everything is hunky-dory. This kind of behavior doesn't help you, the president, or the college, and we don't think it leaves your fellow managers with a lot of confidence and respect in your word or your backbone.

Finally, people are incredibly busy these days, overwhelmed with e-mail and phone calls. To protect themselves and to control the barrage of messages, college staff sometimes put their phones on automatic answering while sitting at their desk. "Sally Jones is busy, but she really wants to hear from you. Please leave your name, a brief message. . . ." So our clients, whether they are faculty, staff, students, or the community, are, in effect, being pushed away and told, "I'm too busy to deal with you." This is not acceptable. It sends a terrible message, especially to someone who may be calling you or the college for the first time. How do you feel when you call the department of motor vehicles, your bank, or city hall and get a "We're busy. Please leave a message"? As a college leader, you need to think about the message you send if you and your staff set your phones to forward all calls to an answering machine. It will not take too long for your college to be known as "We're Too Busy Community College."

BRING OPTIONS, NOT PROBLEMS

A manager who brings a problem to his or her boss without options or recommendations for addressing the issue is really just an overpaid messenger. If the problem or challenge is in your area, you are responsible not only for identifying it but also for finding solutions. The president or vice president should advise you on the validity of the solution, not develop the solution or strategy.

We like working with people who begin their report on a problem or new idea like this: "I've got an idea for increasing enrollment in the social sciences. I've worked on this with my department chairs and have run it by a couple of my fellow deans. I'd like to get your ideas, as well. First, let me outline briefly the enrollment challenge we're facing. . . ."

Change is not an easy thing for human beings. Change agents are not necessarily always your favorite person.
—Bob Herbold, former COO, Microsoft

INSTITUTING CHANGE: EVERYONE IS A LEADER

When it comes to change, we don't practice what we preach in the community colleges. For example, the typical community college catalog includes a mission statement that reads, in part, something like this:

- Our college is dedicated to meeting the dynamic needs of a changing community.
- We seek to empower students to formulate and realize educational goals that will promote their personal growth and facilitate their full participation in a rapidly changing world.
- Our campus will establish, monitor, and evaluate college goals and objectives in relation to the mission and a changing environment.

Despite our allegiance (at least in writing) to change and helping students and the community prepare for new challenges, we tend to resist and even reject change when it comes to how we serve students and do our own jobs. Machiavelli could have been commenting on the prejudice against change in the present-day community college when he wrote in *The Prince*:

> There is no more delicate matter to take in hand, nor more dangerous to conduct, nor more doubtful of success, than to step up as a leader in the introduction of change. For he who innovates will have for his enemies all those who are well off under the existing order of things, and only lukewarm support in those who might be better off under the new.

Anyone on a community college campus can be a leader when it comes to promoting change. It doesn't matter whether you're a custodian, a president, or an instructor, or whether you work in the admissions and records office or sit on the board of trustees. Everyone can be an advocate for change. To paraphrase former House Speaker Tip O'Neill, "All change is local."

For a board of trustees, change is easy: Get a new CEO. Or, better yet, work with your current CEO on definable goals and objectives to promote a new and better way of doing things. For CEOs and presidents, things become a bit more complicated (see "The First 100 Days on the Job," page 56). A CEO or president must build a diverse chorus of people singing from the same songbook as an essential first step. Defining the vision is the first step, but getting others to embrace and articulate that vision on the job becomes the most critical and challenging step in the change process.

Intuit, a pioneer of PC finance and tax software, addressed the need for change by involving a broad cross section of employees. It recruited 10% of its headquarters staff to design a new Internet strategy. The 6 months of deliberations appeared sometimes chaotic, but when the team settled on a strategy, its members became evangelists for change. According to Intuit founder Scott Cook, you need people who have a passion, and you can't order people to be passionate. The same holds true for a community college.

Moving an agenda and playing pool have similar strategies. Sure you can sink the ball, but more important, where does the cue ball end up after the shot? You don't want to just sink the shot. You want to run the table. Smart administrators anticipate and strategize shots—or steps—down the line in order to lay the groundwork for future success. Ask yourself, what will the future consequences or scenarios be from your decision today? How will it affect the various departments or divisions involved? What are the potential political consequences?

Hiring and Managing a Consultant

We like consultants. In fact, we've done some consulting ourselves. Having sat on both sides of table, we know the valuable role consultants can play as well as the problems they can create if not managed properly. What we like best about consultants is they can provide a skill set or experience that supplements the skills already available on campus. They can bring a third-party perspective and experience to a problem that provides the college real value-added benefits in planning, implementation, or evaluation.

The right consultants can also bring with them the moral authority of a "respected outside expert." Former presidents and vice presidents often can make a good living—and provide a valuable service—bringing their moral authority to a college facing difficult problems or needing a fresh perspective on an issue. Here are some reasons for hiring a consultant:

- To validate what you already know needs to be done.
- To bring to a project a specific skill or experience that is not available on campus.
- To be the messenger of bad or politically sensitive news.

This last reason is particularly appropriate for a CEO new to the job who discovers some major weakness within the structure, particularly if it's related to the education program. Faculty are hypersensitive to new CEOs delivering the message that they are not doing a job as well as the last CEO kept telling them they were. It may be smarter not to expend the political capital necessary to get the message out but to use it, instead, to eventually solve the problem (see also "The Theory of Political Capital," page 62).

Consultants can, if properly managed, also say or do something you as an administrator or trustee want them to say or do. We know a CEO who arrived at her new campus and discovered the education program had been happily stuck in the mud for several years. Wisely, she chose not to make the announcement public but to hire a consultant to conduct an analysis of the curriculum, how it was being offered, and its effectiveness in meeting community needs. The consultant became the bearer of bad news, and the CEO expended her energy (and political capital) addressing the solution.

The biggest mistake administrators make when hiring a consultant involves letting the consultant loose without any clear direction or parameters. If a consultant has been brought in to deal with a sensitive, politically charged issue, the last thing you want is a freelancer walking around campus lifting rocks you don't want turned over or bringing home stuff you don't want delivered. Before you bring in the consultants, be sure you know in your own mind what you want. Then when the consultants arrive, communicate those needs clearly before giving them the keys to the campus. Be sure that in your planning meeting with your consultants, you provide them with specifics and details on the following:

- The scope of issue to be addressed.
- What you expect from them.
- The process and techniques they will use.
- Who has editing rights on draft and final reports.
- The campus and community politics involved in the issue being addressed.
- The relevant key players and opinion makers on campus.
- The "no surprises" rule: You want to meet with them regularly to discuss their findings and progress.

Beware of the consultant bearing the "one-size-fits-all" solution. These are the ones who bring to your campus a boilerplate solution they just used at another college that is as similar to yours as the Beatles are to Beethoven. A good way to prevent this disaster is to check all references carefully.

Remember, you don't always have to use their report or abide by their recommendations. You may end up saying to them, "It's valuable information and something for me to think about, but I'm not taking it outside this room." And then you say, in a polite way, "Now, go out and praise the college for its courage and foresight for studying this issue."

ADJUSTING TO A CHANGING OF THE GUARD

When a new CEO comes on board, adjustments are required of everyone who works closely with the new boss. It's a time especially for trustees and administrators to lay aside past practices and open their minds to new ways.

We know a CEO hired by a large district who brought to her new job a philosophy of working closely and openly with all members of the board. Who would object to that? In this case, the new board president. She had just been elected to the chair after 6 years as a trustee watching as the previous CEO focused all his attention on each succeeding board chair. The new chair wanted the new CEO to operate in the same manner. "I've been waiting to be the center of attention," she seemed to be saying, "and now you've changed the rules and I don't like it." The CEO who encountered the unhappy board president needed to meet the problem head on.

Ideally, the issue of how the CEO and board work together as the district leadership team should be discussed thoroughly during initial selection interviews. If a problem persists, the new CEO needs to set aside time with the board to give the issue the attention it requires. A good, clean "takeoff" is in everyone's best interest.

A new CEO also might pose a challenge for a vice president who was an unsuccessful candidate for the top job. This situation can be stressful and threatening to both sides if not handled correctly. Do not run and hide from it. The vice president should take the lead and sit down with the new boss, shut the door, and talk it through. Is this going to work? How are we going to deal with it? Both parties have to be as honest as possible and make some decisions and adjustments.

The smartest thing the vice president can do is to get behind the new president and make him or her successful. Your long-term career aspirations will not be energized or your reputation enhanced by your sulking around campus complaining about the new president. Your colleagues won't respect you. The board won't respect you. And you'll probably just end up cooking your own goose.

The directors and deans on campus play a key role as well in the transition of a new CEO. When a new president or CEO comes on board, people look up the line for signals of how things are going with the new boss. Directors and deans have the opportunity through their attitudes and words to set a positive tone with staff and faculty. A positive comment can give the new president a chance to move the college forward. A roll of the eyes sends a signal that can undermine the new president and college leadership, including your own position as a member of that leadership team.

3

Institutional Politics

We spend too much time arguing over who's going to drive the bus and not enough time thinking about the passengers.
—Bob Jensen

PEER BULLIES

We know an instructor who attended a weeklong, out-of-state conference without authorization from her dean and then bullied her peers into defending her unauthorized absence. The president ordered the dean, who had been on vacation, to write a letter of reprimand and put it in the instructor's personnel file. The faculty member responded by immediately filing a grievance, alleging that the rules for conference participation had been "secretly" changed. The instructor then cajoled several of her faculty colleagues to send letters to the faculty union saying a letter of reprimand was too severe a punishment. Instead of just saying no to their colleague, the faculty members agreed to mail the letters, admitting afterward that taking the path of least resistance was preferable to standing up to a pushy colleague.

Peer bullies come in all shapes and sizes. We were attending a faculty union meeting at a large urban district at which the topic of the funding of health benefits was being discussed. One faculty leader, Joe, argued for taking no action to help administration address the issue. Another faculty leader, Sarah, argued that faculty should work with administration toward a reasonable solution. Joe's reaction was to grab the microphone out of Sarah's hand, jump up on the stage, and attempt to win the argument by literally shouting her down.

We have been amazed at how easily some colleagues are intimidated by those who have no authority over them or who sometimes do not even work in the same department. Often, they know these peer bullies are wrong and probably have only half the story right, and yet they are afraid to stand up and take them on. Why do the bullies get away with it? As we all know, most people do not like confrontation. When an issue arises on which a colleague has few facts, it may be easier to accede to what the bully says or demands than to take the time to research the issue or take a stand that is contrary to union or senate practices.

Many faculty members do not want to get involved in such confrontations. We call them "tweeners": people in the middle "between us and them." Their motto is, "I don't want to be on the senate. I don't have the ego needs. I don't need the stress. I just want to teach my classes and go home." As a result, they leave a vacuum for those who do have the interest, time, energy, and, too often, nonconstructive motives. Peer bullies pose a threat to college administration. Administrators often calculate—sometimes wrongly—that the bully has a big following, so they cave in to peer bully demands. Peer bullies thrive and survive when the administrator doesn't understand the faculty or has no courage.

THE 10/90 RULE

The 10/90 Rule goes like this: 10% of the faculty speak for—or at least try to give the impression they speak for—90% of the faculty. In reality, most full-time faculty members care mainly about these issues in the administrative arena: what they teach, when they teach, what classroom they teach in, whether they get adequate compensation, and office accommodations and parking. Their attitude, and a healthy one at that, is, Get out of my way and let me teach my classes and don't give me a bunch of bureaucratic gobbledygook.

What does that mean for college administrators? You need to cultivate relationships so that you can read the real intentions and interests of the general faculty. Building relationships with faculty helps you understand whether discontented faculty members actually do have a constituency backing them up or are just solo pilots trying to shoot you down.

The best advice we can give is not to cave in when a peer bully threatens you. Faculty members know who the cheap shot artists are among their peers. If they know you know and you don't do anything about it, you'll lose respect. The best remedy? Adopt the sunshine theory. Expose the bullies to the sunshine of facts by being honest and consistent with your colleagues. Bullies thrive by distorting the issues and counting on inaccessible administrators to cache information.

There is something else to watch for as well: the peer bully lackeys. They are easy to spot. They are the faculty, staff, or administrators who sit quietly while you're having an unpleasant confrontation with the bullies and then come up to you afterward and say, "We're right behind you, Sally. We really don't support what that jerk is saying about you. So don't take it personally."

LOYALTY AMONG COLLEAGUES

We knew a campus president years ago who found it just about impossible to work cooperatively with the new chancellor of his multicollege district. It turned out the president had been an unsuccessful candidate for the chancellorship and now was letting his disappointment turn into bad behavior. He took to playing the martyr role acted out by campus presidents in too many multicollege districts: "I tried to get our campus its fair share," the college president would tell his administrators and faculty when he came back from meetings at the district office, "but the chancellor believes the other campuses deserve more than ours." He persisted in his disappointment, eventually turning it into defiance.

Decisions that were agreed on in district cabinet meetings were scorned when the president got back on his campus. Directions the chancellor gave—and the president had accepted—were ignored. Board members heard stories from the campus about how the chancellor, whose office was located off campus, failed to understand campus educational issues.

The punch line to this story came after the president had retired from his job and had applied for a job in a neighboring state. A friend of his former boss, who was a chancellor in the same neighboring state, heard that this disloyal person was now a candidate for a local job and went out of his way to squash the application. He had known the president's management style and didn't want to see this kind of unprofessional behavior move into his neck of the woods.

Loyalty is a valuable asset in community college governance and administration. Without it, trust among colleagues, including the CEO and board team, is nearly impossible. Without trust, the decision-making process is virtually unworkable and long-term friendships are out of the question. Here's our take on how loyalty should flow within our organizations:

Loyalty of the board to the CEO. The board has a vested interest in the success of its CEO and presidents. Their success shines directly on the trustees. Loyalty to a CEO comes from the outgrowth of a successful working, and often personal, relationship between trustees and their top administrator. Good working and personal relations empower the CEO with the mandate of the board to move the college forward, even in tough times or while under fire from critics.

Without loyalty to the CEO, boards are stuck with a high-salaried, do-nothing administrative leader, afraid to make one false move. Furthermore, it's nearly impossible to build teamwork and loyalty among second- and third-tier administrators when CEOs are constantly being criticized by trustees or run in or out of office. Administrators begin asking themselves, "If I get behind this CEO and he leaves, what will happen to me? Will there be retribution against me because I supported the CEO? Will the group who ran off the CEO then come after me?"

Loyalty of the CEO to the board. You work for them. You need their support to be successful. If for some reason you don't respect them, the relationship is doomed, and you had better get out before they catch on. And, CEO, don't go to conferences and bad-mouth your board. If you complain to colleagues about your board, you can just about guarantee one or more of your trustees is going to hear about it eventually from one of their trustee comrades. If you have a problem with your board or a particular member, talk it out face to face. You would expect no less if the tables were turned.

Loyalty of the CEO to administrators. Your team, as we point out repeatedly in this book, becomes your best hope for a successful term in office. Treating its members with respect and compassion will go a long way toward improving your chances of seeing your vision for the institution implemented. Try to build them into a unit (see also "Picking Your Team," page 61) diverse in personality and talent but unified in purpose. Loyalty to their careers and aspirations is a key piece of that puzzle. Please don't punish your entire staff if you have just one culprit. Deal directly with the person at fault. Don't bad-mouth your administrators with other presidents. It's unprofessional and makes you look petty and small.

DON'T FORGET SUPPORT STAFF

The men and women who serve as secretaries, custodians, clerks, technicians, and assistants are invaluable not only to the smooth operation of a college but also to the image projected by the college to students and the community. It has long been our view that, more than any employee group, support staff deserve to be thought of as the most loyal and dedicated employees on campus. Faculty leaders, administrators, and trustees should take care to treat support staff with respect and to encourage staff development initiatives whenever possible.

Secretaries (called administrative assistants in most districts) can make or break you, especially as a college CEO. They usually have a firm grasp on reality, work hard, perform as good diplomats, and possess a sense of history that is invaluable. We've had a couple of secretaries who, if a college education had been available to them in their earlier days, would be giving us orders today. We've had secretaries who could juggle 10 tasks at a time and smile warmly when you handed them another.

But we also once knew a chancellor who berated his secretary, a seasoned pro who had already been on the job for many years when he arrived. His badgering, in fact, forced her into early retirement. The next year she ran for a seat on the board of trustees. Well, you know where this story is going. It wasn't too many years before she was on the majority side of a vote to force his early retirement.

Loyalty of administrators to the CEO. If you can't support your leader's position, you have three choices: Try to change your boss's point of view, support the boss, or get out. In the real world, most people stay put; therefore, administrators must work within the decision-making process, never shying away from arguing a contrary position but ultimately supporting the president's decision. Likewise, don't go into the president's office and bad-mouth a colleague. That's usually not well received by top brass. For one thing, the president might jump to the conclusion that you say the same things about him when you're in someone else's office.

The world of community colleges is a small world. Name anyone who works in any community college in the country and we would bet we know someone who knows someone who knows that person. Our point? Don't carelessly complain about other people. It will inevitably get back to them and end up having an impact on your career—maybe not today but someday in the not-too-distant future. If you ever plan to apply for another job, particularly at another campus, the people to whom you have been rude, disloyal, hurtful, or disrespectful are only a phone call away from the person doing the reference checks. You will find it difficult, if not impossible, to outrun your professional reputation.

CAN IT PASS THE "DO YOU WANT YOUR LOVED ONES TO KNOW" TEST?

Community college administrators, faculty, and trustees face potential ethical quagmires on a regular basis. Tough, complex decisions, conflicting demands on resources and priorities, the quest for power and the need for achievement and recognition, and the sexual tension among men and women working together late into the night and away from home generate innumerable hazards and temptations for the ethically challenged.

We know a college CEO who was propositioned by the board chair. He, the CEO, was single, and she was separated from her husband. After a late-night board meeting, she suggested that instead of going to a local restaurant to have a beer and talk about the meeting, that they go to her house and have a drink. But one thing led to another—the proposition, the acceptance, and the inevitable outcome.

An instructor, desperate to make his class go, enrolled students without their permission and then proceeded to forget what he had done. When he subsequently noticed these students were failing to come to class, he was outraged and gave them a failing grade. His scam came undone when the students complained to the dean after receiving their grades.

A board of trustees hired a CEO to balance the budget and rein in out-of-control employee pay and benefits. When the CEO did her job and employee groups complained bitterly to the board and to the media about the "CEO's lack of commitment to quality education," the board said to the CEO, "Hold it, what are you doing, CEO? People are unhappy! You've got to make them happy or you're out of here!"

A 79-year-old instructor, no longer effective in the classroom but a guaranteed plaintiff in a racial and age discrimination lawsuit if steps were ever taken to force his retirement, stayed on the job. Should faculty, who demand respect for their classroom and education pedagogy, stand up and demand the termination of instructors who are hurting students? What about the instructor's dean? When does inviting a lawsuit become the right thing to do?

We are faced with ethical misbehavior and dilemmas almost every day. No doubt you can cite examples from your own professional experience: faculty who have sex with students, administrators who sell life insurance out of their offices, deans who hire relatives, and trustees who take campaign money from employee groups. The student is an adult, says the faculty member. The administrator is selling life insurance on his own time. And, yes, the trustee pockets the campaign contributions, but she also promises to keep the institution's best interests in mind when voting on employee pay raises. Conflicts of interest? You bet.

You may not be able to teach people ethical behavior, but there is a simple test that will help you spot poor behavior or resist it when it tempts you. We call it the "Do You Want Your Loved Ones to Know" test:

- Would you want your spouse, kids, or parents to read about it in tomorrow's paper?
- Is it how you would want to be treated?
- Is it consistent with your values?

Unethical behavior diminishes the institution and its leadership in the eyes of the campus community and the general public. The college CEO occupies a unique position in the ethical life of the institution. He or she occupies the center of the moral life of the college. How the CEO personally behaves and responds to the behavior of others sets a campuswide standard and example. When he or she behaves ethically and consistently over a period of time, it creates a campus environment that enhances the CEO's ability to make tough decisions on sticky issues and still maintain the support of the campus, even if the decisions are opposed by powerful forces.

SHARED GOVERNANCE: THE CONTRADICTION WE LOVE TO HATE

A college president decided to make shared governance, or collaborative decision making, work on his campus by creating an advisory committee of campus leaders—faculty, support staff, students, and administrators—to review all major issues and make recommendations to the president's council. The advisory committee took him up on his offer, meeting once a week, discussing and debating issues, and struggling with the myriad points of view that major issues tend to generate. Then the headaches began.

When the advisory committee brought its decisions to the president and his council of vice presidents and deans, some of their recommendations were politely but firmly rejected. Rightly or wrongly, the advisory committee members concluded they had been misled. "Why ask for our hard work and opinions if they're going to be dismissed?" they complained. "What do you know that we haven't already considered? Is this shared governance or is this is a benevolent despot? The voice of the faculty is not respected at this institution!" Shared governance—or collaborative decision making—is a continuing tension for many community colleges. The effort to expand the circle of decision makers across the campus raises a dust storm of controversy on the question of where the buck actually starts and stops.

This is our view on shared governance: We believe the board of trustees has ultimate responsibility for deliberating on the recommendations of the CEO and making decisions in the best interest of the institution. Many times we forget that boards, not committees or CEOs, are empowered to hire and fire and make policy. The CEO is empowered to ensure the board receives a comprehensive presentation on the issue under consideration and a recommendation that, if approved by the board, will serve the college well. The CEO also has a responsibility to solicit from his or her administrative staff and the appropriate members of the campus community information, insights, ideas, and opinions on all major issues coming before the board.

One of the greatest weaknesses of collaborative decision making stems from the lack of understanding on campus of how the process works. For that, administrators, and particularly presidents, chancellors, and CEOs, must take the blame. We would be willing to wager that most community college employees have no common concept of how decisions are made and who is involved. That general campuswide lack of knowledge breeds misunderstanding and makes decision makers vulnerable to the second guessers, gossipers, and dissidents.

It is imperative that the institution's board and administrative leadership make clear to everyone on campus how decisions evolve and the roles of the people and groups involved. When campus committees receive a clear statement of responsibilities, expectations, and ground rules, others will have difficulty hoodwinking and manipulating the system.

We do believe in the collaborative involvement of all the appropriate staff and faculty groups, if it adds value. Leave the "two from every group" approach for the feel-good issues. If you are discussing technology infrastructure planning, appoint faculty and staff with technology expertise. If you have more staff than faculty that can bring value to the process, bite the bullet and appoint more staff than faculty. What counts here are results, not politically correct body counts.

What mistake did our friend make by asking his advisory committee to meet and deliberate on all major issues facing the college? Certainly, his intentions were good; however, in this day of raised decision-making expectations, if you appoint an advisory committee and charge them with going through the hard work of studying and building consensus on issues, you had better be prepared to follow their recommendation or take a lot of flak. Human nature being what it is, if you keep asking for advice and then keep rejecting it, you'll be seen either as obstinate or hard of hearing. Be careful with shared governance committees. They have the potential to encircle and outnumber the president, sandwiching him between the committee and his own cabinet and board.

One thing is sure: The campus wallet will take a big "hit" to maintain a multilayered governance structure that includes a president's cabinet with faculty and staff participation; a shared governance committee with faculty, staff, and management participation;

Faculty Peer Review

One issue that does go hand-in-hand with the concept of shared governance is faculty peer review. Faculty members are experts on the subject of learning and teaching and have justifiably argued for years that they should exert primacy over curriculum decisions. It might be assumed, therefore, that faculty members, better than administrators, could assess the effectiveness of fellow instructors in the classroom through peer review.

As a department or division dean, do not expect that to happen. Faculty may believe in the integrity of the teaching profession and the sanctity of the classroom, but when it comes to peer review, few seem willing to expose ineffective instructors and risk opening up a messy debate on standards. When was the last time your campus fired an ineffective instructor, even one that everyone knew was hurting students? Why? Part of the reason is the confluence of interests of the faculty union and the academic senate. Senates, which are responsible for representing faculty on academic issues, often join with the union, which represent dues-paying members on employment-related issues, in a one-two punch against the authority of administrators, even in the case of an incompetent instructor. A dean will find it slightly easier and more effective to single-handedly evaluate the faculty (if allowed by law or policy) and forget trying to insist on peer review.

and budget, curriculum, planning, and staff development committees. Such a structure is cumbersome, and release time for nonmanagers is expensive. (Most faculty would be up in arms if they knew how much release time was costing them in salary and benefits.)

On some campuses, faculty committees are responsible for developing recommendations on curriculum, hiring policies, and even budgets. Naturally, they often see themselves as the legitimate governance entity and believe the president should implement their recommendations without debate or, in some places, even questions. One of the problems with shared governance, however, is that it gives faculty governing power but no accountability or responsibility for implementation. Sometimes even managers buy into this system, which can, in the end, lead to institutional atrophy.

Campus leaders must act to protect themselves and the process by defining decision making and governance, particularly to the faculty. If it means running the college, the answer is no. If it means having input into curriculum, the answer must be yes. Remember: Whoever owns the curriculum process owns the budget. Scheduling determines costs, enrollment, hiring, and, ultimately, budget. Do not give the faculty carte blanche or you could lose control of the heart of the institution.

4

Presidential Issues

Dr. Smith, you have a call on line one." "Who is it?" "He said he's with Heidrick and Struggles." A headhunter, you say to yourself. "Thanks. I'll take the call."

The Call of the Headhunter

You find out the headhunter's calling to ask, to urge, to beg you to apply for a presidency at A Fantastic College. Self-esteem, you have just been rebooted and upgraded with 2 zillion gigabytes of RAM! Talk about a great feeling! But wait. Before you call a real estate agent and the mover, here's a warning and a little advice.

If you received a call about a job opening, especially at a good college, you can bet your next 10 paychecks that at least 10 other men and women heard the same pitch: "This job fits your skill set to a tee, and they're looking for a leader just like you. In fact, [your name here], the job description for this position just about duplicates the great things you've done in your fabulous career. So, [your name here], when can they expect your application? Next week?"

Job hunting is exciting and, of course, a bit nerve racking. So before you respond to the headhunter's call, remember, don't take his plea too seriously. Headhunters routinely either understate or overstate the situation facing you if you do get the job. They will never tell you, "This is a crummy job that will break your heart." Instead they'll say, "This is a challenging job that can be tamed by a top-notch pro like you!"

Do your homework. Take time to analyze as carefully and honestly as possible how your skills, interests, and needs match up with the job being offered and the challenges, resources, traditions, and expectations at the prospective institution. Also, it wouldn't hurt to get a second opinion from a trusted colleague to help clarify your thinking.

If you've applied, let your boss know. We know a college CEO who attended a conference with one of his board members. They were mingling in the hallway when the executive director of the state faculty association walked up and congratulated the college CEO—with his trustee standing beside him—on being a finalist for a CEO job at another district. The faculty leader had no idea he was letting a secret out of the bag, a secret the president hadn't yet shared with his board.

FINDING A GOOD FIT

Okay, you've read this far, and you're still interested in becoming a president, CEO, or chancellor. Obviously, you've ignored our warnings. It has been said that the best presidency you can get is one in which the previous officeholder had messed things up pretty well or was enormously disliked. As they put it in coaching, the best job is often with a team that just went 0–12.

But as we tried to demonstrate in chapter 1, many factors go into deciding whether to become a CEO or president and which type of college you wish to lead. Do you prefer a single-campus college to a multicollege district? What sacrifices will your family make in terms of uprooting yourselves? And, are you ready for the thrills and spills of a top job?

Once you've made up your mind which way you want to go, commit to doing the homework necessary to be a successful candidate. Some of the questions to ask the headhunter and others are as follows:

- Why did the previous CEO leave?
- What kind of board do they have?
- Are there any inside candidates?
- What stage in the life cycle of a college is the district in: Building? Maintaining? Transition? Repair?
- What kind of CEO do they need? Builder? Healer? Status quo? Change agent?

After you're satisfied with the answers, match your skill set against the needs of the district and make an honest assessment as to whether a good match exists. Don't put your line in every stream. If you're fishing for halibut, you don't put your line in a trout hole. For administrators going after their first presidency or CEO job, remember: Many presidencies exist out there for you. Don't take just anything. There are positions out there that are career makers and career breakers. You don't want your first to be your last.

Be persistent. We know a president who served for many years as a chief business officer. To finally become a president, he had to overcome the well-known prejudice against financial officers when it comes to faculty and academic administrators sitting on presidential screening committees. But he did it by building a strong reputation as a statewide leader, not only among business officers but among all types of college leaders. He finished second place several times on CEO job searches before finally finding the right match.

The transient nature of our work makes it possible that you might have been a director at one college, a dean at another, and a vice president at a third. And now you're thinking of taking a CEO position at one of your old haunts. Good idea? Can you go home? It's possible but it can be difficult. The most relevant questions might be whether the campus still perceives you as you were when you left and whether they could accept you now in a much different role. You are not the same person you were back then, and the college is certainly a different place. As the Greek philosopher Heraclitus said, "One cannot step twice in the same river."

Your First Contract

Several years ago a friend of ours was so excited about getting her first CEO job she almost let her enthusiasm get the best of her. She was happily shaking hands with her new board when the board chair, in an altruistic act of unselfish friendship, offered the services of the college's attorney in drafting up the new CEO's employment contract. "Why don't we let old Fred write up the contract for us, CEO-elect. That way we keep it in the family, and it won't cost you a penny."

Bad idea. At this point, big red flags should start waving frantically in your mind. In this case, the contract was negotiated and details worked out. A couple of days later, when the CEO-elect got home and received her copy of the contract to sign, she discovered, upon close examination, that her version was missing some key provisions that had been negotiated. Either the lawyer had made an innocent mistake or the lawyer and the board had unilaterally renegotiated the contract after the CEO-elect had boarded the plane for home.

Get your own lawyer to either help negotiate the contract or at least review it carefully before you sign on the dotted line. Our experience has been that an attorney who helps you negotiate the contract can say things on your behalf that you might not be able to say without embarrassing yourself or getting the new relationship off on the wrong foot. Make the attorney's fee part of the negotiated contract, if possible.

Your first contract represents your best opportunity to get a good contract that will benefit you throughout your career, whether you stay or move from job to job. Don't be greedy, but at the same time don't hesitate to establish the points important to protecting your interests and ensuring that you will be comfortable with your contract a year from now as well as 5 years from now.

Ask to see the previous CEO's contract and copies of contracts of other CEOs in the state. They both represent good starting points on which to build. Also, if in the hubbub of the selection process the board asks you to make a public statement before a contract is signed, simply say, "I'm looking forward to coming to XYZ College upon completion of successful contract negotiations." That puts as much pressure on the board as it does on you to come to a happy and swift resolution.

People don't like to be managed, but they do like to be led.
—Robert Jensen

THE FIRST 100 DAYS ON THE JOB

San Francisco 49ers football coach Bill Walsh popularized the strategy of mapping out the first 20 offensive plays of a game and then sticking to it. Preparation and planning, he believed, were critical to getting off on the right foot. When a change occurs in an institution's leadership, everyone in the institution feels it. It ripples through the system and, like the start of a football game, can cause chaos and surprises.

Problems left unsettled or unspoken will inevitably arise. People will come to the new president to tell him or her their version of the college's past traditions and history, what major issues need to be addressed, how those issues should be handled, and who the good and bad guys are. The new president will hear, "Before she left, President Jones promised me. . . ." or the classic, "That's not how we did it when Dr. Jones was here."

And, as with a sports team, everyone is watching the coach to see what he or she will do, waiting to see who gets put into the game and who gets tossed out. The impression you, as the new president or CEO, leave during the first 100 days may dictate how people perceive you for years to come. It's hard to turn missteps around.

The first step for a new president or CEO is to assess the playing field. A good starting point will be the last accreditation report. Every frog has its warts and freckles, and a recent accreditation report can give you insights into challenges facing your institution and give you license to deal with some sticky issues. (If the stars are all in alignment, your college will be just starting the self-study process, useful as leverage to set your agenda. The accreditation process can also be a valuable tool for improving or implementing a planning process.)

Next, get yourself out of the office and onto the campus and into the community to meet people, establish relationships, and conduct intelligence gathering. We can't emphasize enough the value of the "touch and feel" approach to leading a community college. After all, the term *community college* means the college is part of the community. Meet and interview key staff and faculty and find out how plugged in they are and which ones will be helpful in your effort to move an agenda. Next, find out who the opinion makers are in town and go out and shake their hands and find out what makes them tick. It can be helpful to figure out who in the community holds sway over your board members and whether your board members can actively help you in the community.

After you've completed your initial assessment, the issues, to some degree, will determine your approach. Am I going to play this job for the short haul or the long haul? Am I going to be the change agent needed at this institution, or am I going to run at a pace that will allow me to stay? Some of the issues may be so wrenching that if you do decide to deal with them you know you'll be gone sooner than you may have wanted.

"I thought I was going to be a caretaker," you may find yourself saying, "but it's obvious I'm going to have to be a change agent."

The next step is to build a strategy and, like a coach, develop a game plan to get your college moving down the field. Here are the basic ingredients:

- Set your priorities.
- Now rewrite your priorities, being more realistic.
- Set some priorities that will give you some quick wins.
- Work on selling those priorities to the institution. Organizing a collaborative process that ends up endorsing the same basic priorities you originally envisioned is a sound strategy in this era of shared governance.
- Get your board and leadership team involved from the start.

Look out for board members, administrators, or faculty who say, "We really like you . . . but don't mess with things." Translated this means, "Whatever problems you discover here are problems we are comfortable living with." How to respond? Figure out fairly quickly what those problems are and under which rock they've been buried. Then you can decide which rocks you want to turn over and in what order.

ASSESSING THE BOARD

During the first 100 days on the job, the CEO and the entire board need to come to an understanding of just how they will work together as a team. The CEO must realize, and the board understand, that the CEO works for the board as a unit and not for individual members, even if the individual is the board chair. As the CEO comes to terms with how to work with the board, a critical next step is to find out where the board is—in transition or steeped in the status quo? Is it a low-maintenance or a high-maintenance board? Do board members need a healer or someone to challenge them?

Not too many years ago a college board we were quite familiar with hired a new chancellor to clean up the financial mess. Upon arriving on the scene he found that the faculty had successfully pushed the board to make faculty salaries among the highest in the state.

When the new chancellor identified the problem—pay raises that were beyond the college's financial capabilities—the board was *shocked, shocked* at the news. When the faculty, which had been active in raising campaign funds and walking precincts for incumbent board members, raised a ruckus over the new chancellor's conclusion, the board quickly reached its own conclusion. Obviously, the chancellor had erred.

Reading the board is critical for two reasons: (1) you want to keep your job, and (2) you want to be effective in moving an agenda. To achieve both goals, you need to understand how it likes to work, and you need to be able to assess its probable response to proposals so you can package them in a manner that makes board members comfortable and supportive (and in a way that allows you and the board to not lose face if problems do arise).

There are several steps you can take to help get a feeling of where the board stands:

- Read board minutes and talk to the previous CEO and district "historians" (such as veteran faculty members).
- Check newspaper clippings to see which trustees like their names in the paper and the board issues that generate media coverage.
- Find out who's up for election in the next election cycle and if they have political aspirations beyond the board of trustees.
- Pay attention to recurring themes in questions, comments, and expressed opinions; these can hold important clues about the values and issues of importance to your board members.
- Assess board members' clout in the community and who in the community can push their buttons.
- Meet with each board member individually.
- Assess their tolerance for political "heat."

We know a board that included in its interviews with CEO candidates a unique approach to assessing the candidates' ability to grasp board politics. One of the trustees on this seven-member board would hold up four fingers and ask, "Do you know what this means?" The smart candidate would count the number of trustees around the table and figure out that the board expected its new CEO to respect and respond to the board majority.

Care and Feeding of the Board

Achieving success as a CEO is linked directly to the success of your board of trustees. As such, you must make board members look good as well as help them be effective. It's important to learn about each as an individual, including their professional, family, community, and political interests.

You'll find some board members to be high maintenance and some to be low maintenance. Some want to be taken out to breakfast or lunch every week; others just want the college to run smoothly with minimum conflict. In either case, it can be helpful—and make the job more pleasant—to discover the personal interests of your board members and to involve yourself to some degree in their outside interests. We've jogged on weekends with trustees, attended concerts with trustees and spouses, and sat in bars with others. We've also attended a fair number of weddings, ball games, barbeques, horse races, and Fourth of July picnics with board members.

CEOs use a lot of different strategies to stay in touch with their boards between meetings. One we've found that works well is "The Week That Was" newsletter. We write it as if we're writing a personal letter, giving them not only facts but also insights, trends, potential problems on the horizon, tidbits about staff activities, and our own comings and goings. Such an approach might generate an intimacy that will allow you to minimize the number of necessary one-on-one breakfasts or dinners. (If you like the trustee and his or her spouse, going out to dinner and having social contact is easy to do. But if the trustee is not your favorite person, that's when you have to grin and bear it.)

A common impediment to good CEO–trustee relationships is the trustee who becomes jealous of the CEO's high visibility in the community. This usually occurs when the trustee is not as well known or respected in the community as he would wish. We've known trustees suffering from this affliction to ask the CEO if the CEO could see to it that the trustee was invited to the same parties and community functions as the CEO. Responses include getting the trustee an invitation, not going to the event at all, or not telling the trustee you're going to attend.

Be sure to send the board members all the same board material. Never try to second-guess whether one particular board member would find a piece of information you send to another trustee of interest or importance. Just send it, and let them separate the wheat from the chaff.

> *I never hesitated to promote someone I didn't like. I looked*
> *for those scratchy, harsh, almost unpleasant guys who see*
> *and tell you about things as they really are.*
> —Tom Watson, Jr., former CEO, IBM

PICKING YOUR TEAM

Will your board allow you to select your own team? The point is important because it relates to accountability and your own survivability. As the new CEO, you need the authority to move your agenda, a task made a lot easier and more fun if you have a management team you've blessed—whether you reaffirm the folks that are already on board or bring in some new blood.

But, CEO, a board member might say to you: "The vice presidents often stay longer than you do. For your own protection, we find it imperative that we, the board, help decide who is put in those positions." And you should say right back to the board: "You're right. Selecting the best is important. And I'll make it my highest priority to find the best candidates to choose from. But if I'm going to lead, I have to have a team that follows my lead. You've hired me to get the job done. I can only truly be held accountable if I have a structure in place that makes that possible."

In a multicollege district it's absolutely essential that the campus presidents agree with the chancellor's agenda. We've seen too many multicampus or multicollege districts get sidetracked and chancellors bushwhacked by campus presidents with their own agendas. In a single-campus college, the need to have the vice presidents and the deans on the same page becomes critical. In either case, second-tier administrators who feel no connection to the boss can go through the motions and slow the program down or even stop it altogether.

The first step: Try to make winners out of everyone you inherit. Everybody has his or her strengths and weaknesses. A good leader has the ability to teach and mentor the average performers, those who, if given a choice, you wouldn't have hired yourself but who have competence and are reliable. Any CEO, including mediocre leaders, can fire people. Successful leaders develop the potential in all their people.

When you decide whom you hire or whom you keep, don't clone yourself. Don't surround yourself with people who think like you or have the same skill set. You need to have a sense of what your strengths and weaknesses are and the self-confidence to hire people who complement your inadequacies.

And we're not talking just about professional expertise. If you're an instructional person, obviously you will need a good student personnel dean and business officer. But more than that, you'll also need to find out what the institution needs at this point in its evolution. Look at it from this point of view: Are you a builder, a change agent, or a good maintenance person? If you come into an institution and you're a good maintenance person, but the institution needs a change agent, then you must surround yourself with a few change agents to help you.

When reviewing resumes, the title dean of instruction tells you nothing. We've seen the title assigned to the number two person on campus and to an entry-level division dean at another. Forget the title. In the interview, say, "Show me your college's table of organization and where you sit." That will be far more informative.

THE THEORY OF POLITICAL CAPITAL

A chancellor friend of ours was confronted recently with the startling realization that he had fired the wrong campus president. Not too long after taking over the district, the new chancellor reached the conclusion that one of his four campus presidents was too slow getting on board with the program. No matter what approach the chancellor took to cajole the senior president, he refused to support the chancellor's new ideas. The chancellor subsequently proceeded to expend a great deal of political capital forcing the retirement of this respected but recalcitrant president. A year later our friend came to the uncomfortable conclusion that the real impediment to success was not the president he had dismissed but another president in this multicollege district. By then, other expenditures of his political capital had eaten away at his stack of chips and he was stuck with the real culprit.

Our theory of political capital in a community college may be described in terms of poker chips. Each new president, CEO, or chancellor arrives on his first day with a tall stack of chips. Beginning the second day on the job, that tall stack of chips begins to diminish, whether or not the CEO has spent any on his own accord. If he tries to remove deadwood administrators or rein in expenditures, the chips disappear much sooner. If he moves to alter the curriculum or improve faculty productivity, they disappear almost immediately.

The point? If you need to expend political capital to get something done, such as hiring or firing certain administrators, remember, the time you have the most chips to spend is early in your tenure. Do not wait until that stack is just about gone to place a big bet. Otherwise, you'll have to spend considerable time rebuilding your pile of chips, or worse, time will run out before that stack can be rebuilt.

BUILDING YOUR OWN FACULTY LEADERSHIP

The best faculty leaders and best administrators on your team share some characteristics. They're bright, tough, tenacious straight shooters with integrity, principles, and good communication skills. And, for better or worse, faculty leaders serve as de facto members of your campus leadership team.

The best faculty leaders are quick on the uptake and have a good sense of campus politics. Why? First of all, if they're bright, they get it. They can figure out your ideas and your vision. Get them involved in the decision-making process, because if they're good they'll bring some worthwhile ideas to the table and serve as a counterweight to the conservative types on many campus committees.

We know a faculty leader who inevitably ended up tweaking our ideas, leaving us with about 80% of what we had started with. But it was the most salient 80%, and we figured 80% of something good is a lot better than 100% of nothing. So we went along with him and gave him ownership of the project and, as a result, had a potent salesman inside the faculty tent.

Presidents face problems in finding good faculty leaders, because many presidents don't have a clue as to who the real faculty leaders are. If you're a chancellor in a multicollege district and your presidents don't know, you're really stuck. First of all, the real faculty leader may not necessarily be the president of the union or the senate. It could be someone who has never been an official faculty leader but who may be a bulldog on the issues and, like a good politician, is not afraid to go door-to-door pitching ideas to colleagues.

Get to know your faculty, build relationships, and uncover the bright, savvy, positive, charismatic instructors and encourage them to get involved. If they fit this description, don't worry about whether they agree with you on all the issues. They won't. But if you can't sell the bright ones on your vision, then maybe your vision is out of focus.

LEAVING A LEGACY

The greatest legacy a CEO or president leaves won't be found in architectural drawings or square footage added to a campus but in the men and women the CEO or president hires, promotes, and mentors. The faculty and administrators you bring on board during your tenure will probably teach and lead long after you've left. Their success or failure will be the real bricks and mortar of your legacy.

Between faculty and administrators, which group needs the most nurturing from a president? Well, the most important thing we do is teach students. It makes sense, therefore, that the president of the institution should be intimately involved in the selection of the faculty. In fact, a good case can be made that faculty are more critical to the central core of the institution's success than administrators. Tenured faculty generally stay 20 or 30 years, contributing to the life of the institution and affecting thousands and thousands of students.

CEOs and presidents may disagree, but we say that if you have to choose between spending time hiring faculty or administrators, we recommend you spend your time and energy selecting the faculty of the future. Obviously, the best practice is to find the time to do both.

IGNORANCE IS BLISS, SOMETIMES

An administrator friend of ours once served as chancellor of the same district, twice. During her first go-around, the district faced financial difficulties because salaries in the district were the highest in the state. After she left, the board hired a chancellor to deal with the problem. The new chancellor lifted the carpet, found the dirt, and, to his subsequent chagrin, refused to ignore it.

The board, forced by their new chancellor to examine the dirt, gave a typical board response: "But this wasn't a problem when Jill was CEO." "No," the new chancellor responded, "it was a problem, but she didn't tell you about it." "But we liked Jill. Everyone liked Jill. And no one complained about the problem until you got here. Therefore, this must be a problem you created." The faculty union, which played a major role in the election of board members, eventually ran her out of office. Ironically, the chancellor, who had been part of the original problem, got rehired to get the district "back on course."

Here's our rule: Once you know about problems on campus, you own them. If you don't know they're there, you don't own them. But once you lift up the rug and find the dirt, it's your mess. If you're a caretaker CEO, this may be no problem. You can choose to keep the mess contained and out of sight and still sleep at night. But if you're a change agent, you may not be able to walk by that rug without taking a peek and feel a need (or obligation) to do some housecleaning. If the board doesn't know what problems exist and doesn't have a clear sense of what the institution needs, uncovering the dirt can pose a major challenge for a new CEO—because the board often does shoot the messenger.

Here are a couple of approaches you can take. First, some of us can say to ourselves, "I want to be here 10 years. I don't want to overwhelm the institution by addressing all the problems at once. I'll just look under one rug at a time." That's a good approach, especially for a CEO with a mortgage and three kids to put through college. But here's a better idea that gets the same result: Look under all the rugs and then prioritize the problems you find underneath. Better that you know the whole picture, because how you deal with the first problem you choose to tackle will affect how you eventually deal with the others.

Trustee Election Politics

A board of trustees at war with itself, its CEO, or the college is usually a board that could benefit from some new blood. In states where local citizens elect trustees, the possibility of removing problem trustees through the election process can be a delicious temptation for CEOs tired of unprofessional, destructive, and career-threatening behavior. Keep in mind, however, that sticking your neck out to support one candidate over another in a trustee election—especially if it involves backing a challenger against a sitting incumbent—can be perilous. Obviously, it's much easier for unions to back candidates. A winning trustee opposed by the union cannot fire an entire faculty or support staff.

The best way to approach the task of exorcising an unwanted trustee through the election process is the route taken by the chancellor of a large multicollege district. He went to a friend who went to a friend who was a retired and highly respected former state legislator. The pitch to the retired legislator from the friend of the chancellor went something like this: The incumbent trustee of the college district that serves the community you love has blocked the school's development. The incumbent is not in tune with the education goals of the community. He has become, in fact, an embarrassment to the community and the college district. You are the only possible candidate that can defeat him at the polls and, in turn, save the district.

The approach worked. Not only did the retired legislator run and win, but no direct tie linking the chancellor to the winning trustee appeared. The losing candidate and the other board members could only speculate why such a prominent community leader challenged the incumbent.

You don't want your fingerprints on trustee elections. If you lose, you're dead. And even if you win, you raise the question in the minds of the other trustees: "Well, if he did that to Fred, he may do it to me." Be sure someone else does the dirty work.

Unions may be involved in trustee elections in states where trustees are elected locally. Significant financial incentives may exist for the union to back one candidate or slate of candidates for a board seat, but unions don't always get their way. In addition, even if the union's preferred candidate does win, the trustee may end up having to make unpopular decisions because of financial realities not apparent during the election.

WATCH WHAT YOU SAY OR DO IN THE OTHER UNIVERSE

When you are dealing with people who are power players outside the universe you live and work in and who you think have no ability to affect you or your job, it is best to use the same protocols you use when dealing with powerful people that do work and live within your universe. Powerful people are powerful people. What you do or say outside your universe can come back to bite you where it hurts most. Let us give you an example.

We know a former college president who was at the apex of his career when the congresswoman who represented his college in the U.S. House of Representatives phoned to ask if she could come on campus to film a campaign commercial. As the president took the call, he thought back on all the years the congresswoman had failed to provide the support the college president believed was important to students. When the congresswoman asked permission to film the commercial, the president reminded her that she had, in his opinion, failed the college and that until she took action to support the college's federal initiatives, she was not welcome on campus.

Fast-forward several years to an election in which several protégés of the congresswoman were running for seats on the community college board of trustees. After the election and after the congresswoman's protégés were seated, they formed a majority that quickly removed the president from his position. In many professions, including politics and higher education, memories are long and, in some cases, unforgiving. Don't forget that cold fact of life as you work with people both inside and outside your universe of higher education.

The less there is to fight over, the bigger the fight.
—Pat Kirklin, retired faculty leader and administrator

Votes of No Confidence

In some states, votes of no confidence in the president or CEO have become commonplace. Faculty may view a vote of no confidence as a bargaining chip in pay and benefit negotiations and as a hammer to be used when disputes over major education, budget, and personnel issues reach an impasse. Consider the following scenario. A faculty member commenting on a dispute between faculty is quoted as saying: "He hates faculty, and his priority is not in the classroom." Translation: The union wants a raise. A faculty union president commenting on the board is quoted as saying: "They are not the only taxpayers in this community concerned with educational excellence. There are nearly 1,000 such taxpayers who teach 25,000 students who, too, are concerned about accountability and economic efficiencies." Translation: The union wants a raise.

If the vote of no confidence stems from a labor dispute, the source is usually transparent to the board, and the CEO can usually survive the vote. If it is not the result of a labor issue, a vote of no confidence can be a major problem. In this case, the president should become proactive and take the issue on directly, first by clarifying it and then by taking action toward a solution. If the wound won't stop hemorrhaging or there is no support for the CEO's side of the argument, the CEO should probably meet with the board and negotiate the best possible terms of separation.

The survival rate for managers is much higher than it is for leaders.
—Robert Jensen

Can You Hear the Posse Coming?

When is the best time to leave? The message that you should leave can come in many forms. It might be the board's hesitancy to discuss a contract extension, a trustee's "kidding remark" that your career would flourish better somewhere else, or a subtle but detectable shift in attitude at public board meetings. Maybe your comments and opinions are not always sought—or welcomed. Or worse, the board no longer quickly jumps to your defense at board meetings but lets criticism from the audience linger in the air.

So when should you leave? Sometimes when it would be not only good for the district but also be in your best interest. Frankly, sometimes you've done all you can do and to stay would mean the district will just glide. You may have pushed as hard and as far as the institution will allow.

When a CEO Becomes Ill or Incapable of Doing the Job

Sometimes a CEO will not recognize a health problem that has affected his or her leadership or makes it essential for the CEO to step down. We once knew a CEO who had served for almost 20 years in the top job but who, because of age and illness, was incapable of remembering the names of the people he had worked with for many of those years. When this happens, it is the responsibility of trustees to protect the CEO and his or her family and, at the same time, to protect the interests of the college, its students, and the mission. Trustees should be gentle and understanding, but they must take the appropriate action.

On the other hand, one tried-and-true sign it's time to leave is when everybody's happy and there is no tension present on the campus. Happiness and a stress-free environment usually mean you're not stretching your people or yourself. Another good sign is that no one is raiding your staff or visiting your programs. If no one at other community colleges has much respect for your program, you're probably not moving in the right direction. Or moving in any direction.

CEOs who can stay longer than 10 years have great staying power and are the special ones. If people are clamoring for you to leave, it may not be your fault entirely. You may have made some tough decisions that needed to be made, or the college may have just gotten tired of your bag of tricks and wants a new magician.

5

Not for Trustees Only

Search all the parks in all your cities. You'll find
no statues of committees.
—David Ogilvy, 20th-century business and advertising guru

BECOMING A TRUSTEE

If we were asked to open a trustee hall of fame, we could easily pick a roomful of trustees who, as a result of their wisdom, vision, and dedication, have made their colleges a better place for students. If, on the other hand, we were asked to create a board hall of shame, unfortunately it would be easy to select a roomful of trustees who, as a result of their selfishness, bad judgment, and public spite, diminished their college in the eyes of students, employees, and the community.

Probably the most unsettling time for a college occurs when a new trustee takes his or her seat at the board table. Typically, the concern is not over whether the trustee will demand the college improve or expand its services but the types of personal or political issues the new trustee will want addressed.

If you are convinced you have the answers to improve faculty morale, or evaluate what software the college should purchase to run its fiscal operation, or determine who should get hired for this job or that, don't seek the board seat. And if your goal is to be a full-time politician and you see your election to the community college board catapulting you into the White House, run for the city council instead. Far more city council members get elected to higher office than do community college trustees. Community college trusteeship is often lincompatible with a political career because visibility, controversy, showmanship—attention-getting devices—run counter to responsible college stewardship.

Candidates for a trustee seat should give serious thought to why they want to be on a board. What is their motive? To be a good citizen? To make a difference? To run for another political office? To get something in return, such as health insurance, recognition, or respect? If your answer includes any of the following, you probably have better qualifications to run for the city council or the state legislature:

- "I know what it takes to straighten that place out."
- "I just retired as an employee at the college and am eager to boss the president around."
- "I don't have a job, so I can spend lots of time on campus helping the faculty and staff."
- "I teach at a neighboring community college, so I really know the score."

If, however, you want to be part of a leadership team, a board, and a college focused solely on and dedicated to serving students, then great. Welcome aboard.

STARTING OFF ON THE RIGHT FOOT

New trustees are by their very definition new to the job. They are most likely either going to have some new ideas on how things should be done at board meetings or ideas on campus programs or services. A guaranteed way for you as a new trustee to get a good, commonsense idea rejected would be to show up at your first board meeting and announce that you have completed a study that demonstrates beyond a shadow of a doubt that the college is not being managed properly.

We saw this done once by a new trustee who described himself during his inaugural meeting as the board's watchdog for the taxpayer. The other trustees winced at the not-too-subtle implication that they weren't watchdogs and reacted to his subsequent recommendations with all the enthusiasm of a cat for a bubble bath. Another brand-new trustee we know unveiled a chart at one of her first meetings showing the college had too many managers. She was genuinely puzzled in the weeks and months ahead by the CEO's hostility to her subsequent proposals and questions.

First impressions do count and set a tone for a trustee's success. Examples exist on nearly every college board of new trustees who alienate veteran trustees (often by implying greater wisdom or higher moral standards) and then become frustrated when even their good ideas are ignored or rejected. Nobody likes a know-it-all, especially one who's just arrived on the scene. Human nature tells us we often shun such interlopers, even to the point of rejecting ideas that would be embraced if submitted by team players.

Veteran board members need to remember that new board members are just that, new. Veteran trustees should do everything possible to make a new board member feel welcome. Resist the temptation to say, "We do it this way" or to correct them when a new trustee offers a new idea or makes a public statement that might not be 100% accurate. Show patience, don't be defensive, give them time to learn and to even skin their noses a few times. Embrace them and bring them into the family. Build a relationship based on providing information about the culture of the board and respect for both the mission of the college and the new trustee.

Probably the best rule for new trustees goes something like this: Sit, listen, and keep comments to a minimum. Even if you have a solid grasp of the issues, your goal should be first to build relationships and get a sense of how the board members work together. There will be plenty of time for making your views known. The first few months on the job should be spent plowing the ground so that when you do speak out, people will listen to you as a peer and a colleague and give your ideas a chance to take root.

RABBITS CARRYING THE LETTUCE

We once attended a board meeting where a purchasing issue arose. One of the trustees happened to be an employee of one of the vendors being considered. Instead of stepping away from the table and recusing herself from the discussion, the trustee questioned staff members at length about a competitor's product.

If you do get elected or appointed to a board, remember there is a good reason why rabbits are not trained to carry lettuce. *Webster's* defines the word *trustee* as "occupying a position of trust." Trustees are empowered with significant fiduciary responsibilities, including those related to purchasing, personnel, and budgets. Board members who have direct or indirect conflicts of interest should not participate in discussions or decisions that raise questions of ethical propriety.

For example, board members who take campaign donations from employee groups and then vote on employee pay raises walk a thin line. The constituency of a board member is the community or state, not the employees of the college. Allow us to say that again, because having worked with board members for more than 25 years, we're convinced that many don't get it: The constituency of a board member is the community, not the employees of the college.

Far too often, trustees get on a board and, because they spend so much of their time looking at campus issues involving college employees, they develop an affinity for employees and begin to believe that they are accountable to the employees. This approach to college stewardship completely inverts the oversight responsibilities of lay board members.

Here is another example. The faculty union at one college has succeeded over the years in pushing the faculty pay scale up by getting trustees elected to the board who are willing to pay off political favors. The union, already perceived as extremist, went so far as to back a candidate who was part of the Holocaust denial movement. When the union's candidate got elected to the board and began pushing a pro-Nazi agenda, it was pathetic to watch the union leadership try to defend him. Reminiscent of Harry Truman's sentiment about a South American dictator, the union's defense amounted to "He's an S.O.B, but he's our S.O.B."

The practical result of this analogy is this: Many of the dollars community colleges receive these days are categorical, not discretionary. If they were discretionary dollars, do you think those dollars would go into educational programs? We doubt it. Because of political pressure, a significant portion would go into salaries. That's not to say that people don't deserve to be paid fairly. But there has not been a good balance between the care and feeding of people and of educational programs. Some colleges have dissembled their educational programs to cover salary issues. At too many colleges, politics has put the welfare of employees before the education of students.

Pick Up the Phone

The simplest act of good trusteeship also suffers the most abuse. If a trustee truly wants a good response to a tough question at an upcoming board meeting, the best way to get that response is to call the CEO in advance. In other words, there are no inappropriate questions, but there are inappropriate times to ask a question.

Effective board leadership and oversight begins with open and civil communication between trustees and the CEO. From good communication flows information, ideas, cooperation, trust, respect, consensus, and good decisions. If someone on campus or in the community brings a campus problem to you, don't try to solve it. And don't keep it a secret until the board meeting. Take it to your CEO immediately by telephone or in a private meeting. Don't blindside him or her at a public board meeting with it.

For example, if you have a question about why a particular faculty member or administrator might get hired or if you have information that might be damaging or embarrassing to any prospective employee, call (don't send e-mail, as you cannot be sure the CEO will have read it) and let him or her explain or, if appropriate, withdraw the name until the problem can be checked out. Or, if you receive new information about a faculty union or faculty senate issue coming before the board or receive a call from someone with an allegation of misbehavior, call the CEO before the board meeting and give him or her a "heads up" and a chance to respond or get a response (see also "Loyalty Among Colleagues," page 41).

A CEO who treats his or her board members openly and honestly should be able to expect reciprocity. Conversely, the trustees should expect similar respect from the CEO and his or her staff at board meetings. Here are some benchmarks you can use to judge whether the staff is doing a good job at public meetings:

- Presentations should be kept crisp and last between 10 and 15 minutes. Administrators must resist the temptation to try to demonstrate the depth and breadth of their knowledge by forcing the board to listen to unnecessarily detailed descriptions.
- The presentation should focus on the big picture. That is, faculty and administrators should describe how their program or service fits within the mission and function of the institution.

Selecting the Board Chair

In 1970, the rock–funk band Sly and the Family Stone released the song "Everybody Is a Star." The song includes the line "Everybody wants to shine." When you work with a community college board, it's helpful to keep the song's words in mind. One way to make the dream of stardom come true for trustees is to rotate the board chair position every year. Most trustees want the chairman position on their resume, and just about every trustee wants a turn to shine.

We know most CEOs disagree with this approach. They would rather have their best board member or their handpicked trustee serve as chair, but that sends a signal to the rest of the board that the chair is more important than the other trustees, and that message can end up dividing the board. Several advantages emerge when rotating chair positions, however. For one, we think it makes bad board members better. When every trustee knows it will sooner or later be his or her turn to wield that gavel and have his or her neck out on the public chopping block, trustees tend to behave the way they want their colleagues to behave when it is their turn in the chair.

Also, going through the sometimes bruising board chair election process each year can turn good trustees against one another. Cliques begin to form and memories of past board chair elections can shade the debate and influence voting decisions. Trustees start voting on issues based on who supports whom for board chair rather than on what's good for students or the institution. Keep in mind that seating arrangements at a board meeting do make a difference. Who should sit at the board table? Faculty, students, vice presidents? Contrary to recent shared governance trends that encourage more open seating arrangements, we believe the fewer people the better. You do not see state or federal legislators inviting the public to join them at the table.

Boards invite confusion, and mutiny, if they become too inclusive. Nontrustees, such as the president of the faculty union, might be led to conclude that if they sit at the board table and participate in the discussion, that must mean they are as informed (or more so) as the trustees. And if, like board members, they have a constituency (faculty, staff, students), that is just further justification in their minds that they deserve a vote. Our advice: Keep the board and CEO separated physically from the campus constituencies. It minimizes the confusion and clarifies and elevates the unique role the board plays on campus as stewards of public trust and accountability.

KEEPING A GOOD CEO

We are all familiar with the complaints, warnings, scholarly papers, and hand-wringing over the issue of CEO turnover. Shared governance, tight dollars, and dysfunctional boards have been found guilty in the "literature" and at the conference cocktail hour of driving the average CEO tenure down to about 5 years. We believe that progress toward educational excellence is hindered by a merry-go-round of presidents. If you change CEOs all the time, you never give your college or district the chance to develop and stick with a long-term plan.

If the CEO is moving the college's educational agenda forward, the board should do everything possible to keep that streak going. A board can be effective only if the CEO is effective. Keeping a good CEO is as important as finding a good one in the first place. Here are five cost-free things you can do to keep your CEO happy:

- Follow the "no surprises" rule: Keep the CEO informed and ask questions before reaching conclusions or making public statements.
- Make sure everyone on campus knows that once the board makes a decision and the CEO has been given directions, no trustee will act to undermine the CEO's efforts to carry out board policy.
- Support the CEO when he or she is correct or has been carrying out the will of the board.
- If you hear about a problem on campus, don't try to solve it. Take it to the CEO for resolution.
- Once in a while, say, "Thank you, CEO. You handled that situation well." Good CEOs make the resolution of complex, difficult problems or disputes look easy. As a result, sometimes boards don't understand or aren't appreciative of the behind-the-scenes wrangling, time, and sweat put into resolving tough issues.

Back to the subject of presidential longevity: We also believe that in some cases presidential longevity does not equal a successful tenure. CEOs or presidents who stay 10 years or more may end up treading water; their programs may become stilted and their staff unchallenged. We may be accused of contradicting ourselves here, but we believe that CEO job stability occasionally becomes as big a threat to institutional excellence as constant CEO turnover.

Trustees should be on the watch for too much complacency, fatigue, and insularity if their CEO has been on the job 10 years or more. Complacency and fatigue usually exist as partners in crime. People in any profession can experience burnout, and the president may simply "run out of gas." If the CEO allows the campus to become insular, that is, allows the bureaucracy to become so powerful and dominant that new ideas and initiatives have no hope of succeeding, then the CEO should be replaced.

> *Most of us want to be loved. Scratch that.*
> *All of us want to be loved!*
> —Ray Giles

EVALUATING THE CEO

We were recently talking with a chancellor who has an interesting approach to CEO evaluation. Once a year, at the behest of the board, she sends out a six-page evaluation form to faculty, staff, administrators, and community members, asking their opinions on how the chancellor handles a multiplicity of tasks. This is what business calls a 360-degree evaluation.

We think that's a bad approach. CEO evaluations are important. Getting the opinions of the wide range of groups who work with the chancellor can provide valuable information. But how can a community member respond to the question: "How does the president work with faculty?" How would a community member know?

Customized questionnaires sent to people who have direct (or should have direct) interaction with the CEO can be helpful to boards. The questions should give board members answers that really help them understand how well their CEO is doing. For example, if the board insists the president increase the budget reserve to 5%, and as one result there were no pay raises for the year, the question to faculty and staff leaders might read, "The board demanded fiscal accountability this year. Comment on whether you believe the CEO responded to our directive in a manner that is appropriate to our community college." Another significant question would be, "How well has the CEO responded to the board's goals and objectives for the past year?"

Questions such as "Is the CEO effective in public meetings?" or "Does the CEO relate well to faculty?" may not be as important as the serious question of whether the CEO is moving the college forward as directed by the board. We suggest that the CEO and board chair work together to reach agreement on a format for the evaluation and a series of questions for the board. Each trustee then completes the questionnaire and sends it back to the chair, who summarizes the responses. The board then holds a special closed session with the CEO to go over the summary.

It's at this point that the discussion can become sensitive or tense. Regardless, it's important for the CEO to hear from trustees directly and for all trustees to hear how other board members are feeling about the CEO and the college. Often, a single member or maybe two will have very different opinions about the college and the direction of its leadership. The CEO evaluation gives everyone the opportunity to get an issue on the table and off their chests.

We have seen the situation in which a trustee will make a serious accusation against the CEO that has been festering with this one trustee for some time. The evaluation process gives the board chair the opportunity to say, "When you say he's a dishonest so-and-so, what don't we know that you know? Do you have some information the rest of us don't?"

Another issue of evaluation is whether the CEO should provide the board with feedback. If the board and CEO are operating as a team, both parties need to share how that relationship can work at maximum efficiency. Many times board members don't know that there are a few things they could do—or stop doing—to improve the CEO-board effort. We think CEOs providing boards with feedback is a good idea, but it requires a mature, solid relationship.

CEO evaluation is also a board-ethics issue. If, for example, you ask the CEO to make faculty more productive, how do you expect the faculty to react when it's time to evaluate the CEO? You shouldn't be surprised if they're unhappy. Faculty may assume that it was the CEO's idea and blame him or her. The board's goals and objectives should be clearly stated and publicly acknowledged each year. A key element of board leadership should be the willingness to stand up and publicly state what you expect from your CEO and then stand behind the CEO when he or she carries out your orders.

MAKING THE BEST OF A MISMATCH

When the relationship between a CEO and a board has failed and a separation becomes inevitable, the best advice for the board is to avoid "messing up the nest." You'll need it nice and tidy to attract your next CEO. Remember, everyone is watching. What respected and smart vice president or CEO would want to go to a college (yours) where the board publicly humiliates its top staff? Treat the outgoing CEO professionally and appropriately, which, in part, means in a manner that a potential candidate for the next job will understand and respect. Even if you are angry, the satisfaction of making your displeasure public won't be worth the damage you could do to the institution.

Then, what do you do when there are years left on your CEO's contract? If board consensus dictates that the district would be better served by a new CEO, one strategy might be to privately express to your CEO the board's intention not to extend the contract once it expires. "We're not going to buy you out," you say, "but it would be in your best interest, before our decision becomes public at renewal time, to move on. In the meantime, you'll have our blessings and best wishes in your job hunt. But remember, the clock is ticking."

Don't make your intention public or you'll end up with a lame duck CEO and, as a result, be forced to go to the expense of buying out a long-term contract. If the CEO doesn't get the message or pretends not to hear it, set a deadline, with the stated promise to go public with the board's decision not to extend the contract if the CEO isn't soon out on the job market. Only the most stubborn CEO will fail to see the long-term downside to that option. Separations are inevitable in our business. How you handle them will be critical to the college's image and reputation, in the short term and the long term, and to your image and reputation as well.

SELECTING A NEW CEO

The board's most important job is hiring a new CEO or chancellor. Boards often make several mistakes when searching for new leaders. Here are two big ones:

- Boards too often enter the selection process without knowing the college's needs. As a result, they hire CEOs according to style rather than the skill set needed. You've heard the saying "Boards tend to hire opposites." If they've had an aggressive budget person the past few years, they think they need a sensitive academic leader this time around. If they've been building a

FINDING A CEO FOR A TROUBLED DISTRICT

Is your college in need of repair? Do you want a president who can turn a lemon into lemonade? Instead of making a general search and casting about for anybody interested in applying, we suggest you go out and get yourself a hired gun.

What's a hired gun? A former CEO who is tough, battle tested, and willing to take a year to clean up the mess, take a few body blows, and then get out of town, letting another CEO build on the foundation left behind. Signing up the hired gun as an interim CEO spares the board the time and expense of a general search and means they can pick the candidate with the credentials needed to clean up a messy situation.

Under these circumstances, the board should not only give the interim CEO an ironclad contract but also should expect to be strongly criticized for the tough decisions that need to be made. That's the kind of vision and courage often needed when a district has hit bottom.

lot of buildings, they think the next CEO should be good at consolidating and slowing things down. That's not necessarily the best way to approach the selection process.

- Boards often hire search consultants, thinking that a consultant will guarantee the college a better pool of candidates or a selection process that runs smoother. This may not be the case.

There are four basic steps to selecting a new CEO:

- Determine the college's leadership needs.
- Determine the type of CEO needed to help the college achieve its vision.
- Devise a selection process that will locate and recruit that one-in-a-million candidate.
- Decide whether or not your district needs a search consultant.

Whether or not your district uses a consultant, trustees must know that neither option guarantees success. The preparation work the board does before the search gives a district its best opportunity for a successful search.

To begin with, the board must have a sense of the institutional issues facing the college and what skill set the next CEO needs to lead the college forward. Is the college in the building stage of its life cycle, or does it need to heal itself from past problems? Does it need a change agent or a consolidator? One helpful source for determining your institution's situation might be the last accreditation report. It should help you quickly assess the institution's needs.

Be sure your board is actively involved in managing the direction of the search process and the work of the consultant or lead staff person. Don't hand this responsibility over to a committee. The CEO is the only employee in the district you hire directly. Don't let the selection process out of your grasp.

We recommend that representatives of all segments of the college community be involved in the screening process. (Remember, the stakeholders of a community college are community members, not employees.) Stakeholders will screen applications and conduct the preliminary interviews. Involving representatives of all groups helps promote community and campus understanding of the board's vision for the institution's future direction and helps get "buy in" from the campus for the successful candidate. The committee reviews the paper applications, interviews a large number (15 or so), and then sends a group of finalists—we recommend six to eight—to the board for final interviews.

In the end, selection of the CEO is the board's responsibility. When you set up the selection process, be sure to give yourself the flexibility to consider all candidates you believe would best serve the needs of the college. Make it clear that the board reserves the right to reach outside the group of finalists forwarded by the screening committee. If an applicant didn't make it to the final group but has potential, don't hesitate to ask the committee to interview that candidate. It's your process, your responsibility, and ultimately your decision.

Don't let a screening committee narrow the final group down to two or three finalists. Narrowing the field down too much gives the committee the power to, in effect, select the CEO by limiting the choice of personalities, skills, and experiences. Again, we recommend the board receive six to eight finalists. Invariably, one or more candidates will drop out or references won't check out. You're then left with little or no choice after a long process and feel obligated to hire someone. Not a good scenario.

Don't allow the committee to rank the finalists. This is particularly dangerous. If you give the screening committee that power and then don't select the number one choice, you could face a tremendous political battle and morale problems. For example, if you select number three, four, or five, the one selected may become known as the "second best" or "third best," or worse. Require that the committee bring the finalists to the board unranked.

Does your district need a consultant? We've seen successful searches with consultants, we've seen consultants contribute very little to a search, and we know of situations in which the consultant actually damaged the process. If your district knows where it's going and what it needs from its next CEO, and if it has a reasonably competent human resources office, you can run a successful search without the expense of hiring a consultant.

If your district elects to use a consultant, review "Hiring and Managing a Consultant" on page 33. Be aware that too many consultants bring the same solutions to completely different situations. In the search game, what sometimes happens is that search consultants bring the same list of favorite candidates to all their clients. Sometimes those candidates fit the client district like round marbles in square holes. Having a solid sense of where your institution is heading and the type of leadership needed can help prevent you from accepting a favorite candidate who's wrong for the job. A good search consultant knows the community colleges, has a broad network of contacts, knows the young up-and-comers, and can identify for the board at least 10 strong candidates for the job.

Don't be one of those boards whose members lean back in their overstuffed chairs and say, "Doggone it, we have a great institution. We pay a great salary. All we need to do is open the search and they'll come." Anyone can get on the phone and call every well-respected CEO or vice president and ask them to apply. We suggest the approach taken by big business. Identify CEOs or vice presidents with the experience, skills, and vision that match the college's needs and get the consultant to make sure those people apply. Steal the best brains if you have to. (These are the candidates who probably aren't interested in moving because they are happy and successful where they are.) The board has to be sure the consultant brings a bunch of winners, not just a bunch of people looking to change jobs.

Don't expect that involving representatives of the campus community in the selection process will guarantee campus support for the new CEO. No matter how inclusive the selection process has been, if the CEO is not getting the job done, the campus community will drop him or her like a hot potato, despite being inspected, approved, and given the good housekeeping seal of approval by every constituency group on campus.

Finally, if you can't agree on a candidate after the final interviews, work at it. Don't give up too easily. Selecting everyone's second choice is foolish, even if it means a quick end to your deliberations. In our experience, this has usually meant the district ends up with the second- or third-best candidate for the most important job on campus. We don't believe you necessarily have to reach unanimous agreement behind closed doors on your next CEO, but it is important that when your selection is announced publicly that the vote be declared unanimous so the next CEO comes in with a clear board mandate.

The CEO's success is your success. Give both of you a chance to succeed for the good of the students and your community.

Ten Truths of Community College Leadership

1   **Every decision you make has three elements: educational, fiscal, and political.**
    Too often, we are good on the first element and not on the other two. Too many administrators think, "I'm an educator, not a politician."

2   **No CEO ever got fired for having a lousy curriculum, but many have been fired for not balancing the books.**
    Seventy-five to 85% of our budgets are personnel. Budget is class schedule and student-to-faculty ratio. That's why your vice president of instruction must also understand budgets. If you can't pay the bills, you're gone.

3   **Change is stressful and threatening—and will be resisted.**
    But occasionally, you as a leader must walk the path of most resistance and do what's right.

4   **Organizational conspirators are alive and well.**
    And some of them are wearing the same color jersey as you.

5   **Leadership and management are different skills.**
    We've never heard anyone say that Winston Churchill was a great manager.

6   **Leaders must be self-strokers.**
    If you're looking for a lot of praise, you're in the wrong business. Besides, the people who come up and pat you on the back may be trying to stab you.

7   **There are three sides to every coin.**
    Our job as administrators and leaders is to clarify the ambiguity that dominates so many aspects of human behavior and our or-

ganizations. If you can't deal with ambiguity, avoid the leadership business.

8   **There are no secrets in a bureaucracy.**
This is a hard one for most people to understand. Always give your staff the full deck, 52 cards. Just don't tell them what trump is.

9   **Not all rocks are meant to be turned over.**
If you're the boss, every problem is your problem. But not all problems are meant to be tackled. Cut yourself some slack—let some of the small things slide. As a Zen master said, "The one who is good at shooting does not hit the center of the target."

10   **Community college administration is a contact sport.**
As a leader you should be trying to move an agenda and that means sticking your neck out; when you stick your neck out, inevitably, someone is going to take a swing at it.

INDEX

Aa

academic senates. *See* faculty
    senates
accountability. *See* responsibility
    and accountability
accreditation reports, 57, 84
accuracy of information, 29–30
administrative assistants, 6, 43
administrative employees, xi, 47
administrative regulations. *See*
    policies and regulations
administrative resources,
    allocation of, 13–15
administrators, xi
    adjusting to new CEOs,
      35–36
    bearing bad news, 30, 31
    building relationships, 25
    career progression of, 6–8,
      15–16, 27–28
    choosing to become, 3–6, 27
    communication issues,
      29–31, 34, 77
    in commuter marriages,
      18–19
    ethical issues, 44–46
    functions of, 23–24
    hiring and managing
      consultants, 33–35
    hiring of, 64, 77
    instituting change, 33
    job hunting, 55

    and leadership changes, 58
    loyalty issues, 41–44
    of multicampus colleges or
      multicollege districts, 15
    nomadic lifestyle of, 15–16, 25
    and peer bullies, 40–41
    people skills of, 5, 25–27
    personal privacy of, 17
    political capital theory, 63
    shared governance, 47–49
    team selection, 61
    ten truths of leadership,
      87–88
    See also specific roles and
      issues
advisory committees, 10, 46–49
agendas
    and CEO turnover, 79
    moving of, 10–11, 57, 59,
      81–82, 88–89
    and team selection, 61
alumni, 13
assistant deans, 6
attorneys, and contracts, 55–56
authority and power
    choosing to be an
      administrator, 3
    delegation issues, 24, 29
    and mandates, 42
    moral authority, 33–34
    and peer bullies, 39
    and people skills, 26
    power struggles, 6

Cc

campus autonomy, 10–11
campus committees, 47, 63
campus competition, 13–14
centralization vs.
   decentralization, 15
CEOs, xi
   assessing the board, 58–59
   board elections, 66
   board relationship with, 35–
      36, 60–61, 76–77, 81, 82
   candidate interviews, 19, 36,
      59, 84–86
   communication issues, 30,
      34
   contracts, 55–56, 82, 83
   decision to become, 8–9
   decision to leave, 68–69
   division and department
      leadership, 28–29
   ethical issues, 44–46
   evaluation of, 80–82
   first 100 days, 56–58
   hiring of, 19, 36, 83–86
   incapacitation of, 69
   instituting change, 32–33
   job hunting, 54–56
   legacy of, 64
   loyalty issues, 42–44
   of multicampus colleges or
      multicollege districts,
      13–15
   people skills of, 26
   political capital theory, 63
   presidents compared with,
      9–12

   shared governance, 46–47
   of single-campus college, 9,
      10, 12–13
   and small-town politics,
      17–18
   team selection, 61–62
   ten truths of leadership,
      87–88
   turnover in, 79–80
   votes of no confidence, 68
   See also administrators
chancellors, xi
   advantages and
      disadvantages, 11
   assessing the board, 58–59
   board elections, 66
   CEO evaluations, 80–82
   exposing problems, 65
   finding faculty leaders, 64
   hiring of, 83
   job hunting, 54
   loyalty issues, 41, 43
   of multicampus colleges or
      multicollege districts, 10–
      11, 13–14
   political capital theory,
      62–63
   and service clubs, 13
   team selection, 61
   See also administrators
change
   adjusting to, 35–36
   instituting, 32–33, 56–58,
      62, 87
   of leadership, 56–58
   class scheduling, 28, 49

ethical issues, 23, 44–45, 75–76, 81
evaluations, 48, 80–82
experts, outside, 33–35, 83, 85

Ff

faculty, terminology, xi
faculty committees, 48–49
faculty leaders, 5–6, 54, 63–64
faculty members
  assessing the board, 59
  communicating with, 29, 30, 34
  division and department leadership, 28
  ethical issues, 44–45
  hiring of, 64, 77
  leadership changes, 58
  in multicollege districts, 15
  peer bullying, 39–41
  and people skills, 25–27
  shared governance, 47–49
  votes of no confidence, 68
faculty peer review, 48
faculty senates
  board communication, 77
  first management experience, 3, 5
  in multicollege districts, 14
  peer bullying, 39–40
  peer review, 48
faculty unions
  board accountability, 76
  board communication, 77
  board elections, 66–67
  first management experience, 3, 5
  in multicollege districts, 14
  peer bullying, 39
  peer review, 48
  votes of no confidence, 68
finances. *See* budget and finances
financial officers, 55
firing
  CEO mismatches, 82
  peer review process, 48
  political capital theory, 62–63
  power issues, 6
  and shared governance, 46
  See also retirement, forced

Gg

governance, shared, 26, 46–49, 58
  See also delegation issues
gray areas, 23–24

Hh

headhunters, 53–54
Heraclitus, 55
hiring
  of administrators, 77
  of CEOs, 19, 36, 83–86
  of chancellors, 83
  of consultants, 33–35
  of division deans, 29
  of faculty, 64, 77
  of management team, 61–62
  political capital theory, 63
  and shared governance, 46, 49

board elections, 66
finding faculty leaders, 64
job hunting, 54
political capital theory, 63
presidency types, 10–11
team selection, 61

Nn

negotiated contracts, 55–56
news media, 13, 45, 59
newsletters, 60
nomadic lifestyle, 15–16, 25

Oo

off-campus offices, 5–6, 41
O'Neill, Tip, 32
online courses, 28–29
open-door policy, 26
organizational ladder, climbing,
6–8, 15–16, 27–28

Pp

pay. See budget and finances;
salaries
peer bullies, 39–41
peer review, 48
people skills, 5, 25–27
phone calls, 30–31, 76–77, 86
policies and regulations, 23, 46
political capital, 34, 62–63
political correctness, 47
politics
assessing boards, 59
board accountability, 75–76

and board candidates, 73–74
and change, 33
and consultants, 34, 35
and faculty leaders, 63, 64
institutional, 39–49
legislator relations, 67
multicollege districts, 13–14
single-campus colleges, 13
small towns, 17–18, 19
See also specific aspects
power. See authority and power
presentation guidelines, 77
presidency types, 10–11
presidential screening committees,
55, 84–85
presidents, xi
adjusting to new, 36
advantages and
disadvantages, 11
building relationships, 25
CEOs compared with, 9–12
communicating with, 30, 31
decision to become, 8–9
division and department
leadership, 28
finding faculty leaders, 64
first 100 days, 56–58
former, as consultants, 33
instituting change, 32–33
job hunting, 53–55
legacy of, 64
legislator relations with, 67
loyalty issues, 41–44
of multicampus colleges or
multicollege districts,
10, 11
nomadic lifestyle of, 25

About the Authors

Robert Jensen has been a nationally recognized community college leader for 30 years. He is chancellor emeritus of the Pima County Community College District in Tucson, Arizona, and a visiting lecturer at Claremont Graduate University and the University of Texas at Austin. Jensen is the former CEO of community college districts in Contra Costa and Santa Ana, California, and is past president of American River College in Sacramento. He is a past president of the California Community College Chief Executive Officers and a former chair of the California Community College Commission on Athletics. He has represented community colleges in international education activities in Africa, Mexico, Europe, and Asia.

Ray Giles has worked as a public relations executive at four California community college districts and on the professional staff of three community college state associations. He is currently director of special services to the vice president for the Community College League of California. Giles began his career in newspapers and has written articles for *Community College Review,* the *San Jose Mercury-News,* and *Orange County Metropolitan Magazine.* Giles consults with community colleges on public relations matters and is editor of *Lux Mundi,* the journal of the International Association of University Presidents.